John Stanyan Bigg

Shifting Scenes

And Other Poems

John Stanyan Bigg

Shifting Scenes
And Other Poems

ISBN/EAN: 9783337006198

Printed in Europe, USA, Canada, Australia, Japan

Cover: Foto ©Thomas Meinert / pixelio.de

More available books at **www.hansebooks.com**

SHIFTING SCENES,

AND OTHER

POEMS.

BY

J. STANYAN BIGG,

AUTHOR OF "NIGHT AND THE SOUL," ETC. ETC.

.

LONDON:

WILLIAM FREEMAN, 102, FLEET STREET.

—

1862.

TO

THE RIGHT HON. JOSEPH NAPIER,

(EX-LORD CHANCELLOR OF IRELAND,)

IN TESTIMONY OF RESPECT AND ESTEEM,

AND IN ACKNOWLEDGMENT OF MANY ACTS OF KINDNESS,

AND OF THAT FRIENDSHIP WITH

WHICH HE HAS HONOURED THE AUTHOR FOR SEVERAL YEARS,

This Volume

IS

RESPECTFULLY AND AFFECTIONATELY INSCRIBED.

CONTENTS.

———◆———

PREFACE.

———◆———

ON THE IMPORTANCE OF "ACTION" IN POETRY.

The author of this volume dislikes explanatory prefaces as much as any of his readers. Poetry needs no interpreter; and that which is not poetry is not worthy of interpretation. This, therefore, is not an explanatory preface, in the ordinary sense. It has no special reference to the pieces included in the volume; but as an author of some eminence has chosen to bring forward certain propositions in reference to the absolute importance of "action" in poetry, and as the author of this book does not agree with his arguments and conclusions, he ventures, in a friendly spirit, to offer his own opinions on this matter.

We are not about to attempt a definition of poetry. Whatever it may be, or whatever other attributes it may possess, it is agreed, on all hands, that genuine poetry has the quality of pleasing those to whom it is addressed. This is indispensable, and a test of its genuineness. How is this object to be attained? The purest poetry, say some, is to be written only by ignoring human action. This is to be achieved, say others, only in connection with human action. Action, says a third, is the soul and substance of poetry. Let

B

this be fairly developed, regarding everything else as an intrusion and an impertinence, and then you will necessarily have true and lofty poetry. Let this be wanting, and poetry is an impossibility. With this last, and extreme view of the importance of "action" in poetry, the present writer differs altogether.

Mr. Matthew Arnold, now Professor of Poetry at Oxford, in the preface to the collected edition of his poems, maintains this theory. "What are the eternal objects of poetry," he inquires, "among all nations and at all times? They are actions—human actions; possessing an inherent interest in themselves, and which are to be communicated, in an interesting manner, by the art of the poet." And again he emphatically reiterates the doctrine, that "all depends upon the subject. Choose a fitting action; penetrate yourself with the feeling of its situations; this done, *everything else* will follow." If, it may be asked, the pleasure to be drawn from the perusal of poetry is to be derived solely from the exhibition of noble character through appropriate action, and everything which is not subordinated to this, however beautiful it may be in itself, is to be regarded as an intrusion and an impertinence, why should not verse itself, which imposes unnecessary restraints on the artist, in the execution of his purpose of character-development, be also treated as a like impertinence? If all the pleasure is to be gathered from the story, and none from the manner of telling it, why not tell it in the directest possible way—in simple prose? If, as Professor Arnold maintains throughout his preface, the poet is successful or unsuccessful in his efforts to please in proportion as he is the exhibitor of striking situations, of interesting incidents, of heroic actions, then we would suggest that either the poet or the novelist is a superfluous personage; for the functions and objects of both appear to be identical.

Besides, if "*all* depends upon the subject," then all the poets who have had great subjects, and who have endeavoured to unfold them, regardless of supposed poetical accessories, must have been great poets, and must have written great poems. This conclusion is inevitable. Is Professor Arnold willing to submit his theory to the test of fact? We will assume for a moment that it is true—and what follows? Why, that those whom we have been in the habit of regarding as our greatest bards are in reality nobodies; while a mighty race of Titans, of whom nobody has heard this century, are, in truth, the magnates of our poetical literature. Gentle reader, you are courteously requested to revise your poetical calendar, omitting all the names with which you happen to be familiar, and substituting in their stead the names of those "great unknown," who have written on great subjects, and who have derived their inspiration solely from the themes on which they wrote. Wordsworth, Young, Byron, Keats, Shelley, Thomson, Coleridge, Cowper, great poets? Nothing of the kind! A *fico* for Shakspeare and Milton! Make way for the real grandees—the successors of the mighty bards of old; and keep silence while the herald shouts their names;—Cowley, Wilkie, Glover, and "Poor Pye!" With these "the subject was everything:" and, this theory being true, it follows that our artisans are nightly in the habit of regaling themselves with the "noble action" of the *Davidies*. Our political writers quote their "wise saws and modern instances" from the pages of Pye's *Alfred;* Mr. James and Mrs. Gore were in the habit of embellishing their chapters with mottoes chosen from *Leonidas;* and Professor Wilson must have been quite mistaken, when he supposed the well-thumbed volume in the cottages of the Highlands to be a copy of Thomson's *Seasons*—it was, doubtless, a dog-eared copy of Wilkie's *Epigoniad!*

We agree with Professor Arnold, in thinking that an action that is based upon the primary affections of humanity can never become antiquated. We assent also to his assertion that the date of an action has nothing whatever to do with its interest, and that a great action of antiquity will strike the mind more forcibly than a trivial action of our own times. Nay, we may, without detriment to our own position concede, that "Hermann and Dorothea," "Childe Harold," "Jocelyn," and the "Excursion," leave the reader cold, in comparison with the effect produced upon him by the latter books of the "Iliad," by the "Orestea," or by the episode of Dido. But what then? Does it follow that, because Prometheus, Achilles, Clytemnestra, Orestes, Alcmæon, are more interesting personages than James Jones, John Smith, Thomas Johnson, or John Thompson, "action, human action alone," constitutes the sole attraction of poetry? By what species of logical legerdemain is this conclusion established from the foregoing premises ? Because Homer, Æschylus, and Sophocles evince consummate skill in the development of poetical action, it no more follows that this is the prime requisite of poetry than it follows that all poems must be epics or tragedies.

It is always dangerous to impose the restrictive canons of one people or of one period, on another people or another period, unless it can be demonstrated that the two distinct nations or eras are, in all essential respects, duplicates of each other. Whatever is universal in art and literature, is, of necessity, universally acceptable ; while that which is restrictive in criticism, is generally local, accidental, and temporary. Literature and the arts are not foreign to the soil which cherishes and sustains them. They are the flower and perfection of that people or that era among whom they are born ; but, as nature and humanity are radically the same everywhere, and at all times, and yet are full of endless variety of detail, so that no two scenes, no two nations, no two men, are exactly alike in every particular—so poetry and the fine arts, though working on the same materials, and aiming to produce the same general results, will vary in their characteristics, in accordance with the peculiar circumstances amid which they derive their origin.

Now, no two nations of equal culture, can possibly be more dissimilar in almost every respect than the England of to-day and the Greece of two thousand years ago. This difference extends to almost every particular of climate, scenery, religion, polity, education, morality, and pursuits. The Greek intellect was fond of abstractions, and established its principles of art as it established its philosophy—by processes of deductive reasoning, more frequently than by direct observation of the operations of nature. We should be sorry indeed to endorse what Johnson said to Mrs. Thrale, that "the Athenians of the age of Demosthenes were a people of brutes—a barbarous people." But the Athenian gentleman described by Macaulay, "who might pass every morning in conversation with Socrates, and might hear Pericles speak four or five times every month; who saw the plays of Sophocles and Aristophanes; who walked amid the friezes of Phidias and the paintings of Zeuxis; who knew by heart the choruses of Æschylus; who heard the rhapsodist at the corner of the street reciting the shield of Achilles or the death of Argos"—was, after all, a very different personage from the English gentleman of our own times, who breakfasts in Belgravia, and sups at his shooting-box in the Highlands; who is sipping chocolate to-day by the Falls of Niagara, and a week hence is to be seen walking along Bond Street; who knows what is transpiring throughout Europe, Asia, Africa, and America, and has a summary of the world's passing history laid upon his table every morning; who knows more of physiology than Aristotle, of geography than Strabo, of history than Herodotus and Plutarch; whose library contains more books than Plato ever saw; who sends messages to his friends in Russia and Sweden, and receives replies from them in the course of a few minutes; who wanders amid reliques from Nineveh and Babylon, and is surrounded by the arts of every age and every nation under the sun; who is led by one science down interminable vistas of time, past the abode of the first man, out into a howling wilderness of strange forms and strange vegetation, alive and trembling in the tramp and roar of gigantic monsters more terrible than "gorgons, and hydras, and chimeras dire,"—on beyond the confines of organic life, where the desolating foot of death has therefore never been planted, and out into that appalling silence, never broken save when the primeval thunders spake to each other, when the labouring fires wrought wonders in their terrible caverns and crevices, and the earth shook and quivered like the forests of the ancient oracles, when the spirit of prophecy was on them; who is transported by another science across great gulfs of space, in which suns and systems and constellations roll for ever, and still find ample room—a palpitating wilderness of stars—world on world, system on system, and galaxy on galaxy, until the reason reels, and imagination flags, and the eye of faith alone beholds the pavilion, "dark with excess of light," of that God whom the Greek never knew!

Professor Arnold, after censuring the style of Shakspeare, and citing Guizot and Hallam, in corroboration of his verdict, says, very truly, in reference to the Greek drama :—

"A few actions eminently adapted for tragedy, maintained almost exclusive possession of the Greek tragic stage; their significance appeared inexhaustible; they were as permanent problems, perpetually offered to the genius of every fresh poet. This, too, is the reason of what appears to us moderns a certain baldness of expression in Greek tragedy; of the triviality with which we often reproach the remarks of the chorus, when it takes part in the dialogue; that the action itself, the situation of Orestes, or Merope, or Alcmæon, was to stand the central point of interest, unforgotten, absorbing, principal; that no accessories were for a moment to distract the spectator's attention from this; that the tone of the parts was to be perpetually kept down, in order not to impair the grandiose effect of the whole. The terrible old mythic story on which the drama was founded, stood, before he entered the theatre, traced in its bare outlines upon the spectator's mind; it stood in his memory, as a group of statuary faintly seen, at the end of a long and dark vista; then came the poet embodying outlines, developing situations, not a word wasted, not a sentiment capriciously thrown in; stroke upon stroke, the drama proceeded; the light deepened upon the group; more and more it revealed itself to the riveted gaze of the spectator, until at last, when the final words were spoken, it stood before him in broad sunlight, a model of immortal beauty."

Why, we would ask, should Shakspeare be censured for not adopting a practice whose adoption depended upon circumstances over which the immortal bard of Avon had no control? Sophocles wrote in accordance with the spirit and requirements of his age—Shakspeare with those of his. Why should the example of either be cited against the other? Prominence of details was unnecessary in the case of the Greek dramatist, and would have tended, in the eyes of those who beheld it, to condemn the whole piece :—prominence of details was essential in the case of the English dramatist, and, without it, his whole performance would have appeared bald, vague, and unsatisfactory to his audience. A few electrical words addressed to an enraged mob, or an ardent army already trembling with excitement, might be sufficient to raise the whole to a pitch of ungovernable fury; but an elaborate speech, entering into minute details, might be insufficient to

produce a similar effect on a multitude not similarly
prepared. The outline of the story to be portrayed
by the Greek poet was already in the mind of his
audience. To adopt Professor Arnold's image—the
whole was as a group of statuary dimly seen. What
the poet had to accomplish was to throw light upon it.
But a very different task was allotted to Shakspeare.
He had to hew out the forms, and to provide the
drapery. Attention to "accessories" was, therefore,
in his case, indispensable.

But if it could be shown that Greek poetry fur-
nishes the modern poet with the best examples of the
mode in which action is developed in poetical com-
positions, this would do nothing towards establish-
ing the theory of Professor Arnold—that action or
story is the prime essential, the one thing needed,
in all such works. His reasoning on the matter is
an argument of limitations, proceeding from the
particular to the universal. It should be borne
in mind, that the Ancients wrote poetry to be recited;
the Moderns write poetry to be read. With the
former, therefore, their worthiest poetry inevitably
took an epic or dramatic form, and the development
of the plot was a matter of prime importance.
Undoubtedly, "human actions" are indispensable
both to plays and epic poems; but unless Professor
Arnold can furnish reasons sufficient to establish
the proposition that all poetry is, or should be, epic
or dramatic, he will fail to establish the other proposition, that "human actions" are essential to
all poetry. This, however, he does not attempt to
do. His assumption is, therefore, just as ground-

less as that of Rymer, who said that "Shakspeare ought not to have made Othello black; for the hero of a tragedy ought always to be white." His criticism is just as narrow as that of the other critic mentioned by Macaulay, who said that Milton "ought not to have put so many similes into his first book; for the first book of an epic poem ought always to be the most unadorned. There are no similes in the first book of the Iliad." And his logic is, we think, even worse than that of the facetious actor who reasoned thus:—"All plays are, or ought to be, poems; therefore all poems are, or ought to be, plays!" For, without attempting to prove that all poems should be plays, Professor Arnold would impose upon all poems dramatic restrictions, whether they are plays or not.

It is easy to see whence Professor Arnold has derived his theory. Indeed, he makes no attempt to conceal it. We have already said, that no two nations could be more dissimilar in the mode and extent of their civilization and culture; that no stronger contrast could be presented by any two nations—of both of which it might be affirmed that they were civilized — than that which subsists between Greece and England. And yet, because the Greeks—to whom the art of printing was unknown—wrote poetry to be publicly recited, or for popular representation, and adapted their poems to the purpose which they were intended to serve; the English author, who writes poetry to be read, must adopt the limitations imposed upon the Greeks by the state of their society, and adapt his poetry to a purpose which it was never intended to serve, out of slavish imitation of the Greek masters. The absurdity of such a demand is fully apparent the moment it is stated. Let us extend the same principle a little, and see what will come of it. Baron Humboldt remarks, that the genuine and genial love of nature, for its own sake, first manifested itself in the writings of the Semitic, Indian, and Iraunian nations; and in Europe, in those of the early Christians; such, for instance, as those of Basil and Gregory of Nyssa; while the Greek and Roman bucolic, idyllic, and didactic poems are utterly destitute of it. Is the love of nature, therefore, a thing to be reprehended in the moderns? Landscape painting, as we understand it, was wholly unknown among the Greeks, and even among the Romans. It is true that pictures of natural objects were necessarily introduced into scenical representations, and that, in the Augustan age, landscape painting passed from the theatre into Roman and Grecian halls; but, from the excavations made at Pompeii, Herculaneum, and Stabia, it appears that they were merely a kind of bird's-eye views of seaport towns, public edifices, and villas; and were more like maps than paintings, in which the features of landscapes are carefully elaborated. Are we, therefore, because the Greek painters, like their poets, lavished all their skill on historical and mythical subjects, to burn our Claudes and Poussins, our Rembrandts and Turners, and acknowledge poor Haydon to be the greatest painter since Zeuxis? This, we would suggest, is surely carrying admiration somewhat too far! Boswell, we know, in the heat of his enthusiasm, strove hard to acquire the Johnsonian roll and general ungainliness; and we have heard of certain slender young gentlemen of the last generation—now possibly grown into plethoric aldermen—who carried broken hearts beneath gay waistcoats, and not only cherished Byronic misanthropy, but also carefully cultivated the Byronic limp. Similar enthusiasm carried into the serene region of art and letters, certainly seems somewhat startling, to say the least of it.

The truth seems to be, then, that action, in the all-dominant sense in which it has recently been advocated, is no more essential to the purposes of poetry than the unities of time and place are essential to the development of character in the drama. Those who wish for a story, of the absorbing kind spoken of by Professor Arnold, will not seek it in poetry. They know very well that they may find it in plays and metrical romances occasionally,—almost always, and without the needless encumbrance of verse, in modern novels. The lover of poetry reads poems for something more than the mere excitement of the story. The lover of exciting stories need never read poetry at all.*

---

* It is proper to state that the author communicated the bulk of the above to the *Church of England Quarterly Review*, in 1855.

HARTLEY PIT CATASTROPHE.

Prologue

Written by J. Stanyan Bigg, and delivered by T. Town, Esq.,
Ulverston, at the Concert held there February 11th, 1862, on
behalf of those who are bereaved by the accident.

Death in the Palace; Death within the Cot,
Death in all ranks! 'Tis but the common lot;
He comes with stealthy steps, and in the night,
Taketh our cherished treasure from our sight;
He tracks our steps, through hamlet, tower, and town,
And, with sure instinct, brings his victim down;
And smites the pauper as he smites the crown.
With pallid face he leaps into his car,
And flames out ruddy in the sweat of war;
He comes unto the cottage door and knocks,
And then, in spite of bars, and bolts, and locks,
Some one gets up and goes,—and is not seen—
Only another hillock on the green
Of the Sabbatic churchyard;—all is done,
And one more mortal shall not see the sun!

But seldom to a village doth he come,
Wringing all hearts, and hushing all the hum

Of its glad voices.   Seldom is he seen
Wrapping in shadow *all* the village green;
Seldom he enters in at *every* door,
And writes the fearful legend up—"No more,"
Over the mantel-piece, and on the floor.
No more a father's shadow on the wall;
No more a husband's step, a brother's call,
No more the ruddy child with sunny hair,
Coming into the house—a psalm and prayer.
No more the eager hand upon the door,
For father, husband, brother, are no more.

Thus has it been at Hartley.   Every room
Of every cottage hath its special gloom,
Some one is missing—husband, father, son,
Shall fill their place no more.   Their day is done;
And there is night, and woe, and wail, and gloom,
And saddest shadows fill up all the room
Of the dear lost ones,—each one in his place;
Death hath washed white each bronzed and ruddy face;
And so of all the dearest ties an end,
Of father, husband, brother, child, and friend:
Husbands have said their last "Good-morn," and boys
Have set aside for ever childish toys,
And with the morning breeze upon their breath
Have gone into the mysteries of death,
Their mothers' pleading arms not heeding;—So
Went the grey-headed, so the strong men go
When the dread Angel makes the sign of woe.

A village has been stricken :—On the door
Of every cottage are the words "No more;"
No more the sturdy hands that won the bread,
Husband, and brother, child, and friend are dead.
And we, who come before you thus, to-night,
Cannot bring back the lost ones to the light;
Cannot refill the lorn and empty chair,
Cannot bring back the earnest evening prayer;
Cannot unto the mother give her son,
Nor to the wife her husband—all is done!
But still, amid this holocaust of dead,
The living need what we can give them—Bread!

LITTLE JANE.

———

LITTLE Jane came dancing
Into the sunny room;
"And what do you think, papa?" she cried,
"I saw the father of Ellen who died,
And the men who were making her tomb!
And the father patted me on the head—
All for the sake of her who is dead—
And gave me this doll, and wept, and said
That I was *my* papa's pride."
"And so you are," with an accent wild,
Said the widower wan. "Come here, my child!"

Ah! but her locks were fair and bright,
Oh! but her eyes were full of light,
And her little feet danced in ceaseless play;— ·
"Always be glad, always be gay,
Sing, and romp, and never be sad,
So you will make your papa glad."

And the little one bounded from his knee,
Lifted her doll, and screamed with glee,
As the sunlight fell on the floor;
But who is He at the open door,
Waiting, watching, evermore—
Whose semblance none may see—

Who came unbidden once before,
And hushed the harp in the corner there,
And filled one heart with the wild despair
Of the endless never more?

Stealthy his touch and stealthy his tread,
He lays his hand on her sunny head;—
And who may mention the grace that has fled,
Or paint the bloom of life that is dead?

The present rushes into the past,
Nothing on earth is doomed to last,
Summer has ended and winter is near,
Rain is steaming on moor and mere,
Dead leaves are on the blast.

The shutters are up in the empty room—
Nothing to break its hush of gloom;
Nothing but gusts of plashing rain
Beating against the window-pane,
Mingled with brine swirled up from the sea,
And thoughts of that which used to be
And cannot be, again.

THE HUGUENOT'S DOOM.

———

THE Pastor's house lies in the evening calm;
The cattle are all housed; the labourer's hoe
Rests by his pickaxe; and no sign of woe
Is on the heavens, or on the earth;
For, just as at his birth,
Man sleeps 'mid bloom and balm.
The miller to his 'prentice calls no more;
The child has left his top and marbles on the floor;
The clock is safely ticking on the stair;
And many a pilgrim prayer
Hath knocked, this summer night, at heaven's pearly
  door.

But lo! adown the slumberous hill,
A form is rushing with dishevelled hair,
With straining eyes
That vainly seek the pitiless skies,
Filled with all human ill,
And heavy with despair.
Knocks wildly at the Pastor Fido's door;
And they, within, cry "Go thy way,
Our task has ended with the day;
Wo do not seek for more!"
To whom the stranger cried, with brain distraught,

"Oh! are ye men, and have ye hearts of steel,
That for no human woe can feel,
To whom love's agony is nought?
I tell you I'm the youngest son of five;
And three lie in their gore
Down by the great hall-door,
And Fred and I are all that are alive.
I tell you all the clouds are black with thunder,
And deeds are done to-day, that none may name,
Have wrenched the jaws of heaven asunder, -
And filled them full of flame.
I am the youngest son of five, I say,
And I have seen those sights, and heard those sounds
  to-day!"
"We wot not what thou speakest of," cries one;
"Our task was ended with the setting sun."

Thereat, the stranger gave a cry.
"Open the door," he said;
"And let me see the old man's saintly head,
And warn him, ere I die!"

They drew the bolt; they brought him through the
  gloom
Into the darkness of an inner room,
Where, in his cleric vestments clad,
The old man looked upon the lad.

"O Father!—Pastor Fido!—Holy man,—
O man of saintly eld!"—the youth began,

And choked in tears. "O Father! I have seen
Death-struggles all this day,—
Broad stains of blood along the common way,—
The blood of kindred on the village green;
And sounds of men in agony and pain
Are ringing wildly now within my maddened brain!—
Men!—my own brothers! Murdered in their youth,
And in the flower, and prime, and strength, and truth,
And beauty, of that youth:
They showered their blood like rain
Upon my pathway, as I fled—
The fires of hell all gathering in my head.
Hush! Place thy hand upon my burning brow,
And I will tell thee what has happ'd, and how."

"Calm thee, my son!" the old man said;—
"The sun's hot, crimson stain
Is hardly quenched yet in the distant main,—
Something hath touched thy head."

"Is it the sun? Oh! Old man, is it well
To scoff, and mock me thus? What have I done
That thou should'st gibe and jeer me with the sun?
Hush thee! And I will tell.
Thou talkest of the sun. 'Tis well of thee!
This morn, only this very morn,
I saw him walk upon the ripples of the sea,
And shake his gold out on the growing corn;
I saw him shine upon my father's hall,
Ripening the pears upon the garden wall;

I saw him in my sisters' hair,
And on my father's brow, as the old man bent in
    prayer.
Only this morn, a happy family
Gathered together round that old man's knee,—
My brothers four and I, and my fair sisters three.
And now—to-night—old man!—To-night
The rising moon will show another sight,
Will shine on what the ruthless fires have left—
On desecrated rooms,
On horrible smoking glooms,
On flame-black walls with many a ruin-cleft—
And worse! O God! To-night, the moon will shine
Into my father's cold, dead eyes,—
And into yours, that matched the skies,
Ye three dead brothers mine!"

"Ah! This is sad." "Nay, old man! do not speak.
My tale is short to tell.
These ears have heard a sister's shriek,
And the whoop of fiends of hell.
They came upon us unaware;
We were still upon our knees
When a clatter of hoofs came on the breeze,
And then a hundred feet clomb up the oaken stair.
Lend me thy hand, old man! My senses reel;
Where was I? Ah! the clang of steel,
A hundred troopers in the breakfast-room,
Stabs, groans, cries, curses, then a gloom,

Where grisly shadows swam about
As in some cavern; then a shout
Of horrible triumph pierced my brain,
Mingled with feebler cries of pain.
Old man! Did'st ever hear the like?
Did'st ever hear thy foeman strike
Full on thy brothers' breast, and know
That death was following every blow,
That thou wert helpless, and it must be so?
Hast ever striven, with uplifted hands,
To ward the lightnings from thy native lands?
Hast gathered up thy soul in maniac act
To lift the thundering wall of some great cataract?
Hast heard thy sisters' wail of woe
Clutched by the throat thyself, struggling in vain to
    go?

I saw it all! I heard the hellish din.
I saw the strong oppress the weak—
The weak—my nearest kin!
I saw the deed of blood begin,
I heard its history in my sisters' shriek;
I saw them dropping one by one,
Brother and brother, father and son,
I felt the old man's hair cool on my burning cheek,
As, with a long, low cry,
He fell down stricken by my side;
A keen blade glittered in mine eye,
And then a darkness fell, woful, and deep, and wide.

I cannot tell how long I lay,
I cannot say the sights I saw,
I cannot say the sounds I heard,—
Who can put heart's-blood in a word—
The dearest blood that ever stirred
A brother's bosom?   Well-a-day!
I hardly know, now, what I say."

"And so thy father, the old man, is dead,
And all thy brethren, too, are slain?"

"All?   Said I all?   Nay, all save me and Fred,
And he is coming here amain."
"And wherefore?"   "Nay, I hardly know!
Something about a ship, he said;
And bade me tell this tale of woe,
And save the grey hairs of thy head."
"What of the ship, and what of him?"
"It's riding safely in the bay;—
My mind is weak, my memory dim,
I hardly know what I should say;
But, ere another sun shall shine,
Both he and I, and thou and thine,
Must be at least ten leagues away."

"Ha! ha! my lad, thou speakest well;
A ship is riding sure enough!"—
The laugh was cruel—the voice was rough—
The speaker flung aside disguise—
But worse than laugh, or voice, the eyes

Looked up, two ruddy pits of hell !
And the youth saw, in wan despair,
It was a trooper fierce and fell—
A face and form he knew too well—
That sat in the Pastor's oaken chair !

" Old Pastor Fido sails to-night
In the galley-slave ship in the bay ;
And thou shalt join him ere the light
Dawns on another day !"

AN IRISH PICTURE.

A SMOKING swamp before a cottage door;
A drowned dog bobbing to a soleless shoe ;
A broken wash-tub, with its ragged staves
Swimming and ducking to a battered hat,
Whenever the wind stirs the reedy slime;
A tumbled peat-stack, dripping in the rain ;
A long, lank pig, with dissipated eyes,
Leading a vagrant life among the moors ;
A rotting paling, and a plot of ground,
With fifteen cabbage-stalks amid lush weeds ;
A moss-grown pathway, and a worn-out gate,
Its broken bars down-dangling from the nails ;
A windy cottage, with a leaky thatch,
And two dim windows set like eyes asquint;
A bulging doorway, with a drunken lean ;
Two half-nude children dabbling in the mire,
And scrambling eagerly for bottle-necks ;
A man akimbo at the open door,
His battered hat slouched o'er his sottish eyes,
Smoking contented in the falling rain.

SHIFTING SCENES.

Proem.

TO MY WIFE.

WELL, dear! our little world is hushed and still,
And the great world is far away, as we,
Sitting together, on this tranquil night,
Pause in our talk, and think a little while,
And look into the fire, and see the past
Unfold itself, and all its scrolls flash up
In sudden sparkles of swift thought.

                    Our boys
Are in their cradles, safe and well; and dreams
Are filling both their baby-hearts and souls.
Our eldest child was with us as we walked
Over the hills, and through the woods to-day,
For the first time;——his little trotting steps
Falling on both our hearts, like music heard
When heads are bowed, and the cathedral chant
Goes up to God on faltering steps of prayer.
Here are the sticks I cut for him; and he,
With the imagination of a child,

Pronounced them tall as trees; and, in his hands,
They towered up lofty as the Alpine pines——
Our little darling Jacky!—Hope and pride
Of both our hearts.

　　　　　　And little Harry, too,
Is lying in his cot—our "two-year old"—
With smiles dimpling his little happy face
Into angelic sweetness:——Bless them both!
"Grandpa" has said "Good-night," and all is hushed;
You, sitting at your customary work,
Ask for a story.　Well, then, take these lines—
The echo of a legend from afar,
A winter dream of southern summer-time,
A medley of the distant—and the near;
The present—and the past; and if you see
The moral that is hidden in the tale,
Then will the tale be dearer for its sake,
Although it is not branded on its front,
Nor made to dance attendance, everywhere——
A lackey to the story through the whole——:
'Tis a love-offering:——Take it then as such!

I.

ABSENT.

SCENE: *A Garden near the Royal Palace. Time,
Evening.* HAYTI, *the Wife of* JUG DEV PURMAR,
is walking alone.

HER eyelids droop; her cheek is wet;
    And all its budded roses blow
    Fainter, and fainter still, and grow
Like lilies white, and whiter yet.

Her happy babes, that all the day
    Ran up and down the garden-walk,
    And filled the air with their dear talk,
In a sweet slumber softly lay:

Her glorious babes—so bright and fair—
    She almost wonders, as she sings,
    They do not spread out gauzy wings,
And soar into the summer air.

Their laughter is so rich and deep,
    She links it with the songs of birds;
    And all their little lisping words
Come trembling to her in her sleep;

And all the light of their sweet eyes
　　Is garnered in her heart of hearts :
　　She often thinks with shuddering starts,
They are bright aliens of the skies ;

And trembles, lest some holy night,
　　A glory-form should break the gloom,
　　And, shimmering through their little room,
Take them for ever out of sight !

So wondrously their faces burn,
　　So purely dance the sudden gushes,
　　She often thinks the tell-tale blushes
For some more radiant planet yearn ;—

Somewhere beyond the gleaming bars
　　Of sunset, on a golden even—
　　Somewhere—she knows not where—in heaven,
Whence comes the spirit-peep of stars.

Her one sweet boy, so merry and wise,
　　And her two dainty little girls,
　　Shining behind a dance of curls,
That dazzle the mother's loving eyes,

And give her heart-beats, as she sees
　　The floating glory glimmer and break,
　　Like rippled moonlight on a lake,
Through the cool darkness of the trees.

Like streaming moonbeams, through the boughs,
     Lending a lustre to each other,
     The loved twin-sisters and their brother
Go gleaming on with brightening brows;

And into her heart of hearts they go,
     With all their laughters and their wiles,
     Their innocent words, and happy smiles,
And all their life's unsullied glow,

Awaking dim imaginings
     Of happy isles and regions tender,
     Where beings of supernal splendour
Glide hushing through a gleam of wings;

And faëry palfreys come and go
     From castles hid in hoary woods
     By faëry streams, where falling floods
Fall silent as the falling snow.

And now each baby calmly sleeps;
     Her happy nest is warm and well;
     Why should her bosom heave and swell?
How is it the beaming mother weeps?

Her stalwart husband's at the war,
     And tongues are false, and friends are few,
     And kings are mortal, and the true
Can meet no charges when afar.

II.

ENEMIES AT COURT.

Scene: *An Apartment in the Palace. Present,* Sidh Raj, *the* King; Ameer, *and* Sivar, *Conspirators, and Enemies of* Jug Dev Purmar.

Sidh Raj.

He lies who says that Jug Dev is not brave!
Thrice have the breezes borne his banners home
Scorched in the breath of battle, ragged and torn,
Crimson with carnage, but victorious.
Thrice have the eager messengers rushed up
The forest avenues, with straining eyes,
Crying to all the winds the note of conquest.
Thrice has he gone down into the garden of Death,
And torn up victory by the bloody roots.
His bickering brand has beaten back the hosts
Of the on-coming fate that threatened us
Three times; and as a storm goes through the woods
Shaking their ancient empire like a leaf,
And tumbling the grim giants down in heaps
Of grey dishevelled ruin, even so
Did he go down imperial to the foe,
And they lay strewn and wasted.

AMEER.

Good, my lord
The King speaks true. No man denies the might
And valour of Purmar. They have been proven
In battles endless, both abroad and here;
In camp and palace, by the river's marge,
And in the imprisoned darkness of the forest;
In broils of his own seeking—at the court
Of him to whom his fealty is sworn.
His aim is sure; his arm is mailed in might;
His step is doom; his very look is death.
He is a very Azrael to our foes;
But, may it please the King, his wings are long,
And flap the blood of kinsmen in our face!

SIDH RAJ.

Ha! The old story?

AMEER.

Not so old, my lord;
But every child in Rájput, ten years born,
Remembers, shuddering, how the brave Jug Dev
Slew the King's brother in the open day.

SIDH RAJ.

He well deserved his fate:—his doom was just.

AMEER.

The King is very merciful. The world
Is less so.

Sidh Raj.

Ha!　Sir Dark-face, of the thin
And shrivelled sneer, with its pale treachery
Dancing like death-lights on thy cruel lips!
I do believe the breasts that gave thee suck
Were bitter with the bite of aspics, that
Thy veins run thick with poison 'stead of blood,
So wicked are thy words, so pinched and worn
Thy looks, and such a fire of hellish hate
Glints deadly-bright through thy half-closed lids,
Like the live levin leaping through shut clouds.

Sivar.

Let not the King be angry!　Ameer speaks
What thousands hold imprisoned in their breasts.
He is too bold, perchance; in the face of his king
He should seek courteous terms, and silken speech,
And keep the rude and ragged garb of truth
For plainer presences, and lighter talk.
His loyalty is greater than his wit.

Sidh Raj.

Do ye all mock me?　What is't ye would say?
No fear of Ameer's prudence!　He would plant
One hand upon his bosom, and with speech
All tender sleekness—Devil's milk and honey—
He would come sidling up unto his friend,
And send the hot blood hissing to his eyes,
A dagger in his heart!

> Away with you,
> Base time-servers! that just have courage to crawl
> Behind your monarch's chair, and whisper fraud
> And treachery against his bravest friend,
> Who fights his battles and your own; defends
> The homes which you could not defend; hurls back
> The coming ruin; props your roofs;
> And hunts the hungry wolf away that laps
> Your very children's blood!
>
> Slaves that ye are!
>
> So tanned and rubicund! So free of speech!
> All plump as sun-stained berries in the woods;
> While he seeks famine just that you may feast,
> And, with his arms, buys freedom for your sons;
> And is paid back in slander.

AMEER.

> It is well
>
> The King should spurn his slaves. And yet—

SIDH RAJ.

> And yet?

AMEER.

> The King hath friends as true, though with less
>   thews,
> Less brawn and muscle than Jug Dev Purmar:—
> With less blood on their hands, of friend and foe:—
> Friends who ne'er bullied the Monarch to his face,

Nor slew his brother in the open court,
Nor scored their bravery on their country's heart.

SIVAR.

The tiger-cat is brave who tears our kids;
The lion is no coward, though he kills
And munches in the dark.

SIDH RAJ.

                    What ho!   Our friend
Is a poor warrior simply; not much skilled
In the sweet speech of courtiers; does not serve
Rank meat on silver platters; nor brim up
A golden goblet full of poisoned wine;
But gives you homely fare and honest speech,
And so has done with it.   Your daintier selves
He cannot rival in luxuriousness:—
He knows it well;—be satisfied.   He fights
That you may feast; he toils in sweat and gore
That you may dally through a summer day
With the light wenches in the laughing woods;
He wrestles in the bloody billows of war,
And grips the hard and bony hand of death
That you may mingle in the merry dance,
And lap the sweets of lips more ruddy than wine.
His deeds are rough—his speech is like his deeds—
And this hath angered you.

SEVERAL COURTIERS.

If we might speak,
Not for ourselves, but for our Monarch ?—

SIDH RAJ.

Then
You would drop poisoned honey in his ears,
Say loyal things with most disloyal hearts,
Claim all our trust with treachery in your souls,
Speak honest-sounding words with lying lips,
And, while a falsehood festered on your tongue,
Pay eager deference, outwardly, to truth.
Bring in a robed and jewelled skeleton,
And let the royal diadem blaze up
And burn above his white and ghastly brows ;
Bow down in worship; hail him as your King ;
And give him sceptre o'er your rotten hearts :—
But as for him ye wot of—he is true.

AMEER.

If the King would but listen to his slaves—

SIDH RAJ.

He would hear slave's-talk ;—not a doubt. What
    more ?

AMEER.

'Tis said, he whispers that a day will come

When Rájput shall bow down her haughty head,
And take him, on his own terms, as her king.

Sidh Raj.

'Tis said too, my good friend, not long ago,
A certain pampered courtier, menial-like,
Lifted his eyes up to that Queen of Love,
Hayti, the spotless wife of brave Purmar.
'Tis also said the Warrior met the Chief
Gay in his flaunting feathers and his silks,
And sadly spoiled his plumage! Nay, 'tis said
That, in that hour, the gaudy butterfly
Shook all the gold-dust from his shining wings,
Slipped off his purple down, his burning bronze,
His velvet spots, and all his ruby rings,
And was a wasp thereafter. Was it so?

Ameer.

My lord the King is pleasant.

Sidh Raj.

                    It is well
Ameer thinks so!

Sivar.

              My lord! If I might speak—

Sidh Raj.

But to what end? Full well I know thy speech,
From its first stammer to its rounded pause.
What! is Sidh Ráj so weak that he will give
His mighty war-horse to the wolves, because

The foolish dogs go baying at his heels ?
Or shall he cast his trusty brand away
Because a slave has dared to breathe on it ?
And have ye all forgotten who it was
That, in the hour of deadly peril, saved
Your monarch's life, while you stood white as trees
That have been barked by lightning ?

Ah ! that day,
That was a blush of fruits and fluttering wings—
A rich delirium of sounds and odours—
When every breath was balm, and the great cusp
Of the bright heavens gleamed with gorgeous gold,
And all the forest was a trembling thrill
Of blended music, and of odour-rain,
And we, with all our train, went out and danced
Beneath the quivering boughs, and in our sport
Flung the ripe fruit, half-bursting, at the girls ;—
When in upon our merriment there broke
That grand and gleaming terror; with his eyes
Burning their sockets in the lust of blood,—
The hungry lion, flaming on his prey,—
And his mane rolling billows of stormy fire,
And ye shrank back, and whitened in the blaze
Of his fierce anger—when, as suddenly,
A flash shot through the hot and sultry gloom,
And in the midst of us, even like a god,
His great brand dripping gore, and all his soul
Hurried in crownèd crimson to his face,
Stood Jug Purmar !

Ameer.

But, my good lord and King—

Sidh Raj.

And even now, hath he not left his bride,
With all her budded beauties in rich bloom,
To battle for our kingdom ?

Ameer.

Dearer than bride,
With all her jewels warming on her breast,
Is the rich prize he seeks.

Sidh Raj.

(Not heeding the interruption).

And hath exchanged
The eager clamour of his happy babes,
Who with plump fingers patted his swart cheeks,
For the shrill shriek of war, the sudden stab,
The crunching blow, the terrible death-grip,
And the fierce wrestle on the slippery sands,
Sodden with gore !

Sivar.

He fights the best
Whose stake is heaviest in the bloody fray ;
And he who sees a sceptre in the mirk,
May edge his shoulders through a world of foes.

AMEER.

He who walks over slaughter to a throne—

SIDH RAJ *(to Sivar)*.

Thou never didst love Purmar, hoary friend;
And yet, O Sivar, I have known thee lay
Great burdens of applause upon his back.

SIVAR.

I might cry " mighty " to the glistening force
Of the sleeked torrent, as it glided by,
With all its hurrying waters gathered up
And marshalled for the dread and terrible plunge ;
But if I saw a pale face gleaming white
Amid the snaky blackness of its folds,
And going ghastly down the ebon wall,
I should look on with horror evermore.

SIDH RAJ.

Thou hast not spoken, Ali : What sayest thou ?
Thy heart is gentle, and thy words are wise.

ALI.

I would say simply this, my noble King,
That, if the pillars that support our roof
Be given to shaking, why the roof may fall.

SIDH RAJ.

A fool's speech truly! Is there nothing more?

SIVAR.

And the same shoulders that prop up the throne
Have power to hurl it, with its pearlèd state,
And all its purple honours, to the dust!

III.

THE WARRIOR'S BABES.

SCENE : *The Forest near the Garden.   Three Children
playing.*

THREE little babes are laughing
    In among the trees,
Six little eyes are dancing
    Glad as summer bees,
In the cool of leaves, in the gleam of springs,
    In the shadow and the breeze.

Trailing golden garlands
    With many a tug and bound,
Breaking off the blossoms,
    Showering odours round ;
With a laugh, and a shout, and a clap of hands,
    Purpling all the ground.

Through the tangled forest,
    By the river's brim,
And through the crouching mosses
    Beneath the arches dim ;
With faces bright, and with hair like light,
    They go with ruddy swim.

Still laughing and still crushing
   Berries in the rout,
Tossing up their garlands
   With merry laugh and shout;
Through the sun and the shade with a sudden skip
   Bounding in and out.

And, where the holy silence
   A sandalled pilgrim stands,
And communes with the forest,
   In hushed uplifted hands,
In the wild sweet glee of their infancy
   They break the solemn bands,

And carry all their gladness
   With sudden turns and dips
Down the dusky silence,
   Into the deep eclipse,
Till the grim woods laugh, and the gnarlèd boughs
   Bud out in eyes and lips.

IV.

IN THE FIELD.

Scene: *The Camp between the Opposing Hosts.*

All splashed with bloody foam, the heroes stand.
Three stabs have weakened Purmar, and the blood
And gore well freely.   Two swift blinding blows
Have lopped the flesh from Afrah ; and still hot
And fierce the battle rages.

      Three set times
Did Purmar come before the opposing hosts,
And challenge any hero to the fight ;
But they, beholding his majestic mien,
His towering height, and mighty strength of limb,
And knowing well the prowess of his arm,
Returned no answer.

      Till grim Afrah rose,
The dread of Rájput: Snake-like in his scales,
Writhing, the warrior came, and glowed and gleamed
With hate and envy.   Both their blades leapt out
At the same moment, and both bickered bright
Over the heads of both the eager hosts,
Whose faces paled with passion where they stood.
Both the swart heroes fought in rings of fire
As the sun flamed upon their burning brands ;

A moment more, and both their blades ran blood.
With his keen dagger Afrah stabbed the side,
And brought the Rájput hero to his knee;
Who, on his feet once more, hurled high his brand
And smote slim Afrah on the shoulder-blade.
Afrah, impatient, closed upon his foe,
Relying on his pliancy of limb,
And strength compacted in the smallest space,
Hurled high the Rájput warrior; every nerve
Beat as a pulse of fire; and every limb
Ran down with lightning as they tugged and swerved;
Both their huge shoulders burst in knotted wreaths,
Like rings of serpents writhing in the fight;
The earth shook under them as down they fell,
Afrah beneath, and Purmar on his foe;
And all the thirsty wildnerness of sand
Drank mighty draughts of blood. Blinded with gore,
Each seized another weapon.   Afrah first
Aimed a fierce blow at Purmar's bleeding face,
Which, parrying, the Rájput hero swung
His terrible war-club, knotted like an oak,
And brought it down with all his giant force
On the tall front of Afrah.   Down he dropt,
Like a huge monarch of the forest, struck
By thunder, 'mid his peers; and all the host
Of Rájput, that had stood in silent awe,
Broke, like a loosened torrent, into shouts
Of wild acclaim.
                          Meanwhile, Purmar, half blind,

Beheld a gleam of lances as he reeled
On to the camp of Rájput; and a swirl
Of giddy smoke floated 'twixt him and heaven;
And all the distant forests and blue hills
Span round and round in ruddy wheels of light;
And heads and faces of the army near
Danced as on rippling water; broken glints
Of far-off shining rivers, green of leaves
Sun-touched, and aching wastes of dreary sand,
With ghastly faces lighting up the mirk,
Whirled, in a roaring chaos round his head,
As on he staggered to his tumbling tent.

V.

THE LONELY WIFE.

Scene : *A Room in* Purmar's *House.* Hayti *alone.*

All day in purple sat the sun
  Amid his sumptuous train ;
All night the pale moon, weird and wan,
  Wandered through clouds and rain.
All day the winds, like laden wings,
  Dropt odours rich and dim ;
All night they shrieked through groaning boughs,
  And caverns dark and grim.
All day the hills were crown'd with light,
  Light laved their shining sides ;
All night the torrents roared and dashed
  Their black and sunless tides
Through thunderous glooms and avenues
  Of ghastly ribbèd rocks,
Whose every pallid bone of flint
  Shuddered beneath the shocks.
All day the sun-crowned forest thrilled,
  And hummed with bee and bird ;
The tiger and the lion roared
  All night, and were not heard ;

So fiercely shrieked the murderous storm,
   So wailed the shrill winds thin;
With such an angry shout the heavens
   Tumbled the darkness in.

My day is done, and, like a flower,
   Folds all its sweetness up,
The wine of life is rudely dashed
   Out of the golden cup;
And all the sunny hours, flower-wreathed,
   That danced upon my floor,
Have taken all their garlands off,
   And sing and dance no more;
My day is done, my sun has gone
   Down to a weary bed;
The night comes shuddering down the heavens—
   The night—with all its dead!

I look into my children's eyes,
   I stroke their shining hair,
I kiss their little ruddy lips,
   I see *him* budding there;
I go about my household tasks
   Blindly, with eyes down-bent;
All night I ask my aching heart
   How the long day was spent;
All day I wonder when the night
   Will come to cool my brow;
Both night and day I thrust my arms
   Through the barred dungeon—now.

I cannot rest.   Some greedy want
  Eats all the light away,
And on the pearlèd bosom of sleep
  Gnaws at my heart alway.
The daily heavens blaze like brass
  Above my burning head;
And then the shuddering night comes down—
  The night—with all its dead.

I see the first pale streak of dawn,
  I see the giant limb
O' the sun stride o'er the bars of heaven
  Out of his dungeon dim;
I see the shadows gather and leap
  In their evening thunder-race;
I hear the night-winds howl and moan
  Up in the moon's pale face.
No rest have I at night or morn,
  For evermore I see
The red surge creep, the red waves leap
  Up in a bloody sea;
And evermore a great fear comes
  Swooning across my soul,
As I hear my husband's well-known name
  In Death's dark muster-call.
Sometimes I hope; a little space
  The sun shines through the rain;
But soon the gathering blackness comes,
  And then I grope again

Through charnel-damps, by reeking walls,
　With darkness overhead—
Touching the cold and crawling things
　That batten on the dead.
O heavens! I would I only knew
　If I a widow be :—
Sometimes I clutch my happy babes,
　And cry—" My orphans three !"
They only smile up in my face ;
　They only clap their hands ;
They fling their blossoms at my feet
　And skim along the sands.
Sometimes, in self-deceit, I bring
　His quiet evening meal
And listen—not a bird can fly,
　Nor drowsy beetle wheel.
But I can hear it :—oh! I hear
　The midnight midges hum,
And listen till the stars burn out,
　But still he does not come !
I know he will not ; yet no leaf
　Nor blade of grass can stir,
But through my heart a wildering rush
　Goes with a giddy whirr,
And dashes all the fevered blood
　Up to my heated brain ;
I cannot bear it ; but I sit
　And listen yet again.
Sometimes a lonely footstep comes

Along the crispèd grass;
I cry with joy, and through the door
   Bewildered burst—alas!
It is to feel two shining eyes
   Burn in upon my brain;
And go like serpents o'er my wounds
   With poison to my pain:
I hoped for Purmar, but behold
   The wild and wicked leer,
The deadly hate, the deadlier lust,
   The fiend-smile of Ameer!
I shut the door, I wring my hands,
   And something wrings my soul;
For, by the present drear I see
   The golden past unroll;
But something sends a deadly smoke
   O'er every sunny scene,
And all its crowned and regal joys
   Shrivel to phantoms lean;
And all the present agony
   Pales o'er its beaming brow:
I cannot, though I struggle, leap
   Out of the seething now.
My day is done, my sun has gone
   Down to a weary bed;
The night comes shuddering down the heavens—
   The night—with all its dead!

VI.

AT COURT AGAIN.

SCENE: *An Inner Room in the Palace. The conspirators,*
AMEER *and* SIVAR, *together.*

AMEER.

THE poison 'gins to work. The wine of victory
Already blackens on his parchèd lips.
He shudders at the shout of conquest.

SIVAR.

Ay!
His glances flame as they would shrivel up
The gladdened crowds, who come with eager eyes,
Crying, "Another battle won!" even as
After long droughts, and on the windy nights,
A fire goes roaring through the forest boughs.

AMEER.

He sees his diamonds dimmed in his own blood;
He sees the hand of Purmar on his crown
Fingering its jewels, and his shadow flung
Black as a death-pall o'er his tottering throne;
And every wind that carries home the news
Rustles with doom.

SIVAR.

I saw the clouds of doubt
Gathering when last we spoke together.   He
Pooh-poohed our foolish arguments, as one
Who, after a ghastly dream, hears the interpretation
And finds it dark as death.

AMEER.

He joys no more
In Purmar's triumphs.   We were as the seers
Who make the same sign which the phantoms dread
In midnight mystery made beneath the moon,
And utter, in broad daylight, the weird words
He heard the ghostly voices whispering low.

SIVAR.

He laughed at all our warnings as one laughs
Who hears the steps of ruin in the dark
Coming to meet him.   All his words of trust
Were wrung from him, like drops of agony.

AMEER.

Had he not doubted first, our silly talk
Would have fallen light as April rains
On the thick walls of serried adamant
That front the sea ; but now a whisper shakes him.
He starts aside as though he were suddenly stung
By some fierce serpent-thought.   In festive hours

His looks grow dark, as though he saw a hand
All white and ghastly pluck the garlands green
Off the bright brows of all the laughing girls,
And painting pallid death-signs on their cheeks.
His old victorious banners whistle doom
Flapping above his throne.   Down his vast halls,
In all their gloomy gorgeousness, he walks
As though he saw a sudden dagger gleam,
Poisoned and pointing at his royal heart.

SIVAR.

Let's nurse these visions up to the maddening point,
When he will dare and do.

AMEER.

     No heavy task!
Leave him alone and all his nightly dreams
Will swarm with lean hands beckoning but one way.

SIVAR.

The cup already winks before his eyes;
Frame an excuse, and he will drain it dry!
He hates the name of Purmar now;
And all the noise of battle in his ears
Gathers in tempest for his special head.
What are the foes of Rájput now to him?
Triumph is but an ugly mockery
Whichever way it falls.   The victor-wreath,
In any case, is rank and foul with death.

AMEER.

But what a sorry fool is this, to doubt
His best friend at our bidding, thus;—to "cast
His trusty brand away, because a slave
Has dared to breathe on it:"—These were his words.

SIVAR.

He hath most royal notions of Purmar.
He talks of sceptres as of baubles, poor
In such a grasp; kingdoms were but as shells
Laid in so wide a palm; and diadems
Would gain great lustre on so grand a brow.
He hears his name shouted in ecstacy
On every wind of heaven.   He sees his plumes
Tossing in triumph through the thick of war;
And in his ears the chariot-wheels of fate
Go thundering through the dust of coming years,
With Purmar holding by the golden reins.

AMEER.

We must strip off this gorgeous cloth of gold,
And place a beggar's weeds upon his back;
Whisper base trifles in the warrior's name,
And rob the hero of his heroism;
Pluck off his gear, and pin a whirligig
Upon the big brows of this wooden god.

SIVAR.

The lion singed is but a sorry beast!

AMEER.

To look at, truly! We must trim his claws,
And draw his teeth.

SIVAR.

And then, when all is done;
When we have slighted all his victories,
Trampled his broidered banners in the mire,
Tarnished the lustre of his mighty arms,
And all befouled his white and spotless fame,
And cloaked the hero up in infamy,
Then will the hatred of Sidh Râj break out
Unchecked by fear, and then—

AMEER.

Good-bye, Purmar!
And then for scornful Hayti.

SIVAR.

Ay, and then,
When this gigantic bugbear is no more—
We need not boast nor bully, but may say—
Monarchs have sat more safely than Sidh Râj!

—◦⟨⟩◦—

VII.

FAR AWAY.

SCENE: *The Garden;* HAYTI *singing.*

AH! the heavens are too high,
    And the sunshine, and the light,
        And the purple mountains far,
        And the moonbeam, and the star,
    And the round and rolling white
Of the sun-cloud, sailing bright
Through a sea of molten light,
    And the shows of day and night
        Seem not what they are!

Evermore a glory breaks
    Over peak and over plain
        In the distance, far away;
        And the gorgeous skirts of day
Hide the hollows full of pain;
Hide the rents, and hide the rain;
Hide the dark funereal train;
Hide the clouds that come again;
    But no living thing can say .
    It hath touched the gorgeous day,

Which for ever, and for ever,
Glideth on, a golden river,
　　Far away!　Far away!

Evermore there bursts a bud
　Which may never come to bloom;
　　Evermore, in cloudy car,
　　Beameth up some royal star,
　　Which some evil thing may mar;
　Evermore the summer seas
　Shake in light; the laden trees
　Stoop in glory to the breeze;
But the beauty of the flower,
　And the lustre on the sea,
　And the glory on the tree,
　　And the radiance of the star,
Are not star, nor tree, nor flower,
Yet of that, which, hour by hour,
Lendeth them their golden dower,
Who may know it?　For the flower,
　　Star, and sea,
　　Bud, and tree,
　Seem not what they are!

Evermore a crimson dawn,
　Or a glory-swimming noon,
　　Or a night as bright as day—
　　With a never-ending play
　　Of beaming star and moon—

Gladdens all the heaven with dreams,
Gladdens all the earth with gleams
Of forgotten things, and streams
   Dimpled lustre on the river
     Far away;
But for ever all the glory
Of the never-ending story,
   And for ever, and for ever
     All the bright and ceaseless play
     Of the sunbeam,
     Of the moonbeam,
   On the tree-top, on the river,
   Are for ever, ah! for ever,
    Far away! far away!

VIII.

FRIENDSHIP.

SCENE: *A Private Room in the Palace;* SIDH RAJ *alone.*

GREAT acts beget great thoughts, great purposes,
And noble aims; and he whose deeds transcend
The deeds of kings, has kinglier aims than they.
Shall he, then, who has trodden down all ranks
In high endeavour, for the sake of rank,
Fall to the bottom of the lowest abyss,
And be a kingless king through treachery?—
Shall he, whose life has been a constant growth
Of all unselfish virtues, of high aims,
Suddenly shrink, until the very dwarf
Who conjures to the rustics in the woods
Might write "black traitor" on his princely brow?
I'll not believe it!
           There be those who say
The hand that grasps a sceptre need not mind
The blood that purples on the royal palm;
But is he one of these? And are the rags—
The merest emblems of regality—
So precious that a royal soul should fling
All that is kingliest eagerly away
For their sake merely? Then were he discrowned

E

The jewelled diadem blazing on his brow;
Then were he sceptreless although the gold
Of royalty burned hot within his hand;
And then were he, the kingliest soul alive,
Suddenly beggared, though an empire flung
Its kingdoms at his feet, and though his robes
Trailed on the marble floors of palaces.

He, whom foul wrong has placed upon a throne,
Has sorry subjects! He who rules through crime
Rules none but criminals. All are not kings
Who wear the robes of royalty; a slave
May don the purple, and be still a slave.
Shall he, who is a king by right, be less,
And break his golden sceptre on his knee
For a mere beggar's bauble red with blood?
He would not bring this stain upon his soul!
My old familiar friend!—my counsellor!—
My heart, and hand, and soul—my more than brother,
Who hast in endless conflicts shed thy blood,
Hast led my armies, won my victories,
And been before me, like an uncrowned god
In every grand emprize—uncrowned because
Greater than crowns and empire,—shall I plant
My foot upon thy neck at last, and feel
Thee dwindle, till a monarch's cloak can hide
In its starred folds all thy nobility?
Shall I grow large in death, and thou grow less
Than any honest beggar in the realm,

Though sitting on a throne?

                        Nay! Shall I doubt

Thy pure high-mindedness, because I wear

These robes, and slaves are fawning at my feet?

IX.

WHERE ARE THEY?

HAYTI *alone in the Garden.*

DREAMS! dreams! dreams!
Ah! the gush of morning
 Reddening all the streams;
Ah! the smoking mountains;
Ah! the leaping fountains
 Drinking in the beams;
Ah! the golden tassels
 Of the forest hoar;
Ah! the gush of glory
 Breaking evermore
On the forest, with its gums
 Pouring incense at the gate
 Of the dawn, where, clad in state,
 All the sumptuous menials wait
For the King who never comes!
 Whither, whither
 Goeth all this dance of light,
 When the trembling lids of night
Shut upon the heavens? Ah! whither

Goeth all this dance of light,
All this marriage-robe of white,
    Whither? Whither?
Ah for ever! Ah for ever!
    They are dreams.

Dreams! dreams! dreams!
Ah! the ripple-silvered sea,
Ah! the blooms upon the tree,
Ah! the whirr of bird and bee,
    And the music of the streams;
Ah! the plumed and painted play
Of the golden-robèd day
    With his quiver full of beams;
Ah! the ripple and the shiver
Of the sleek and shining river,
Ah! the tremble and the quiver
    Of the crimson flower-gauzes,—
    Ah! the music and the pauses
        Through the day;
Ah! the shimmer and the glimmer
Of the blossom-laden boughs;
Ah! the whimple and the dimple
    Of the laughter-haunted brows,
        Where are they—
    And the crimson of the rose,
    And the evanescent glows
    Of the bud that never blows,

Where are they—
When, from out the black and riven
Tent o' the swirled and swinging heaven,
Leaps the Storm-King with his levin,
  Where are they?

X.

THE CONSPIRATORS.

SCENE: *An Apartment in the Palace.* SIVAR *and* AMEER *in conversation.* ALI *breaks in.*

ALI.

WELL, have you heard the news?

AMEER.

What news?

ALI.

Nay, then,
I see ye have not! Certain schemes have failed.
The mesh of cobwebs, friends, hath given way.
The lion is at large once more, and soon—

AMEER.

What lion and what schemes?

SIVAR.

Nay, friend, speak out;
Leave riddles to the idle. In a word,
Is't well?

ALI.

All's lost! Your schemes are nought but smoke.

AMEER.

Speak, man! What is it? Have the ancient gods
Broken the silence of a thousand years
To warn or favour him thou wottest of?

ALI.

The war is over. Purmar's coming home!

AMEER.

All's lost, indeed, then!

SIVAR.

               How is this? Was not
The messenger in time?

ALI.

               He was, to meet
The army wending homeward, rich with spoils,
And drunk with victory—banners and plumes,
Chariots and horsemen gleaming in red gold,
And clamorous with conquest:—Heaps of gems,
And skins, and slaves—captives of high degree,
And princely trophies of his prowess brings
The chieftain to the monarch.

AMEER.

And the lad?
He did not say his message?

ALI.

But he did!
Aye, word for word.

AMEER.

The fool!

SIVAR.

All's lost, indeed;
And we, I fear, with all!

AMEER.

What! told Purmar
To change his tactics, with that laughing crowd
Of old victorious faces looking on,
And heaping petty insults on the chief
Whilst triumph blazed about his hated brows
In every conquered banner?

ALI.

Every word
The stripling breathed into the warrior's ear
Of his commission.

SIVAR.

Aye, and more, no doubt?

ALI.

No doubt!

AMEER.

Then let us hope the message thrilled
The hot hate of Purmar through every vein :—
Our triumph may be yet.

ALI.

No fear of that—
No hope, I mean! For I am told the lad
Spake of the love of Sidh Râj, and revealed
The state of things in Rájput.

AMEER.

Traitor! Ha?

ALI.

Who? Where? The lad? Aye, maybe so.

AMEER.

Aye he
And others nearer!

ALI.

Youngster have a care!

SIVAR.

Nay, spare your breath friends; you will need it all.
Hath the king laughed at us ? What does it mean ?

ALI.

He was sincere. He doubted his old friend,
Thanks to your hints.

AMEER.

And yours.

SIVAR.

Already, ha !
Is this black fruit, recrimination, ripe ?
Peace ! We are all embroiled; and if so be
That Purmar will forgive the royal fool,
So much the worse for us. His hate will fall
Sharp as his blade upon our plotting heads !

AMEER.

We'll wait and see the issue; if advèrse,
Then for the sunny jungles of the south,
And farewell Rájput.

XI.

HOPE.

Hᴀʏᴛɪ *in the Garden, singing.*

Aɴᴏᴛʜᴇʀ day!   Another day
  Cometh in cool and calm,
With flashing rills, and music-thrills,
  With bee, and bud, and balm;
Adown the heavens he traileth light
  And crimson as he goes;
And all earth's nestlings, eager and bright,
Purple and pallid, blue and white,
  Their daintiest hearts unclose;
And a flutter of homage greeteth him,
And a garlanded glory meeteth him,
    And a dance of springs
    And a rush of wings
  Go with him as he goes!

Another day!   Another day
  Showering from on high,
In bright attire, in car of fire,
  Burneth along the sky;

And every dew-cup, to the brim,
   Trembles with wine of gold,
And, caught in silver, with a swim
Of purple and azure, rich and dim,
   Go mists o'er wood and wold;
And a song leaps up like a thing of light,
From the hush of the woods, half drowned in night,
And a flashing wing dips darkly bright
From out of the cloud that saileth white
   With him o'er wood and wold,
      And a blush of bowers,
      And a dance of flowers,
   Litter his path with gold.

Another day! Another day
   Cometh in cool and calm,
With flashing rills, with music-thrills,
   With bee, and bud, and balm;
And now no more the weary rose
   Lifteth her head in vain;
In his burning kiss her red lip blows,
In his look of love her red cheek glows—
   She hath caught his fiery stain;
And the purple tufts where the violets are
   No longer stir and sigh—
"Oh! the Day, the Day, in his golden car,
And his crimson robes—he flames afar,
   But he never cometh nigh"—

For they feel him on their veinèd tips,
They feel him on their dusky lips,
  He flames up in their eye.
And a drowsied odour shimmer,
And a mellowed purple glimmer,
    And a whirl of white
    And a dance of light
  Go with him gleaming by.

Another day !　Another day
  Cometh with cool and calm,
With flashing rills, with music-thrills,
  With bee, and bud, and balm;
And into my inmost heart he goes
  With bird, and bud, and beam,
And every withered blossom blows,
And every thorn sprouts out a rose,
And every waste-place gleams and glows,
  And brightens like a dream;
And a thousand love-caresses
Shake out their silken tresses,
  And dance along the way,
Where the bliss-bud bloweth,
Where the day-dawn goeth,
Where the life-stream floweth
  For ever and aye;
And all the dewy splendour
Of the passion strange and tender,
With its silent, sweet surrender,

Is with me now alway,
    And faileth not,
    And paleth not,
With the pale and fainting day.

XII.

VENGEANCE.

Scene: *Outside the Royal Palace, wherein the* King
entertains Purmar *and the Victorious Captains:—*
Ameer *and* Sivar, *together.*

Ameer.

Now is the time for vengeance.   Every hour
Rolls the doom onward.

Sivar.

          Aye! the wine will mount,
And then the dark tale will unfold itself,
Before the gaping crowd, and then the ire—
The terrible ire—of Purmar will break out
Fiercer than fire.

Ameer.

          Ere that, we'll see what fire
Will do to quench it!

Sivar.

Are you ready?

AMEER.

Yes.

The faggots are besmeared, the train is set;
But I shall wait until the midnight hour,
When all the wine of revelry is red
And runs in riot through the festal halls,
And then a fiercer flame than burns the brim
Of sparkling goblets shall surprise them all,
And fold them warm in fiery winding-sheets!
Just at the midnight hour, we light a spark
Shall make a bonfire of Purmar; and all
The warriors who have "gained our victories"—
And Sidh Râj with the rest—feathers and all,
Plumes, purple robes of state, and crown, shall be
Cinders to-morrow! You will join me then?

SIVAR.

I will!

XIII.

NEMESIS.

Scene: *The Palace.* Ali *has beckoned* Sidh Raj *and*
Jug Dev Purmar *outside.*

Jug Dev arose,
The monarch following, out into the air
Where the night burned with all her cabbala,
With her star symbols and her mystic calm;
All unobserved as yet.   The revelry
Went on, but dragged a weary weight.   The jibes
Fell dead and stale, and all the merriment
Trod on the skirts of dark forbidden things,
And passed like pageant past a place of tombs
When all the midnight flambeaux flame and flash
Full on the ghastly emblems.   Every voice
Had whispered undertones; and every laugh
Was bitter at the core; and though the wine
Ran ripe and red, it warmed, but did not cheer.
Some secret seemed to lurk beneath each word,
And all the conversation rippled on
Like conscious waters, in whose ooze and slime
The uncoffined dead lie white, with glazèd eyes.
Portentous silence drew about the hall.

Each soul sat brooding in a ring of night,
Wherein no step unconsecrate might tread;
Some special terror leered with fiendish eyes
In at the window of each separate heart,
And knocked with ghostly warning at the door.

When, in a moment, all the paled lamps fell,
Sputtering their jets of fire, whereby each saw
White faces leaping ghastly through the gloom,
As all his neighbours rose upon their feet.
Then three sharp shrieks, like deadly daggers,
    stabbed
The silence:—Out into the breezy night
The revellers hurried through the open door,
And, looking up, beheld the stedfast heavens
Ruddy with stains of fire, and all the far
And dusky mountains staggering through the night,
To meet the fire-king in his furious raid.
High up, the palace was aflame. And there,
Perched on the topmost tower, in agony
Clutching each other were the traitor pair,
Ameer and Sivar; for some unknown hand
Had prematurely kindled the first spark
That caught them in their own thick mesh of fire.

And now the red and roaring surge updashed
Its flaming spume about the buttresses,
Shot up its tremulous tongues of forked wrath,
And grew and gathered round the fated tower;—

Its inpent fury bursting through the rents
And broken fissures, leaping on the night.
Hot lips of flame kissed the black cornices,
Blue jets of fire hissed through the crevices,
Fierce crested waves curled inward, dashed and broke
In glittering spray about the battlements,
Horrible cones shot up into the heavens,
Thin snakes of flame span out into the night,
Long sweeping billows flung their fiery froth
Full on the blistered front of shrinking walls ;
And still the two forms, black amid the glow,
Loomed high above the red and rolling sea,
That now retreated, now roared out amain
In threefold fury, with its fiery waves
Lusting for conquest ; till, at length, the beams
And rafters bent, and broke, and fell ; and then
With a long roll, the mighty fabric lurched
Shuddering inwards.

        All the hollow glooms
And dark domains of night, that had been filled
With the fierce splendour, all the startled hills
That on their crests had felt the ruddy glow,
And all the beasts of prey, from holes and dens,
Sank back into the dark, and disappeared,
As silence once more fell upon the night.

XIV.

AT HOME.

Scene: *The House of* Jug Dev Purmar.

Time, Evening.

HAYTI.

And shall I wake the children?

PURMAR.

    Let them sleep,
And I will look on them. All the home-joys
Come fluttering their warm welcome to my soul,
Joys all too long estranged, which, in the heat
And hurry of war, draining the heart-blood dry,
Seemed sad and distant as the pitying moon
To him who sees her as the ship goes down
Amid the boiling surf, lashed white with rage,
And recollects the dewy tender time
Of tears and kisses underneath her beams
With the sole maid he loves. Ah! I have stood,
Falchion in hand, and stayed the deadly stroke,
Thinking of wives far off, and helpless babes,
Dreading to put the hated name of death
Into their innocent prattle;—turned away,

Lest haply some small childish voice should say,
In aftertimes, with wonder in its eyes,
" My father's dead, slain by the great Purmar,
Who made so many orphans long ago ! "

Down the red path of slaughter, littered with death,
Thou and thy little ones came hand in hand
With most melodious steps, and healed the wounds
Of ghastliest anarchy, and sounds of woe.
In the war-fever, when the blood was high,
And all the shadowy halls of sleep ran red
With gore and carnage—rang with fighting men,
And the strong horror of the tug and strife,
Ye came upon me like the breath of spring,
Murmuring along the grass and early leaves,
And flowers sprang up with deep ambrosial cups,
Full of cool nectar and delicious dew.

While I was wounded, lying in my tent,
The noise of battle clanging in my ears,
A feverish sleep came o'er me ; and I stood
Hard by a mountain, black and thunderous,
Which, as I gazed upon it, cracked i' the midst,
Broke into hollow caverns, jagged and dark,
Whence came a noise as of a gathering host
Of trampling millions from the nether world,
That boomed and thundered through the black abyss,
Until at last the hideous van appeared :—
They were the dead of countless centuries

Who had been slain in battle. On they came
With all their gaping wounds shedding new blood,
And the white woe of deadliest agony
Dashed on their upturned faces, on the which
The moon, hanging between two thunder-clouds,
Shed pallid lustres, weird, and sharp, and wan.
Eagerly upward welled the wondrous waves
Of this great human sea; and all that came
Were as the waters in a sandy creek
To the on-coming ocean still behind,
Its mighty volume rolling thunderous,
And wide, and dark, with slow and sullen swell.
Thousands on thousands wound from out the gloom,
Crowding on tumbling thousands. Heads came up
Livid and ghastly through the welling wounds
Of the tormented mountain, gleaming white,
Followed by countless myriads, till the plain
Ran o'er and weltered with the thickening throng,
And all the little hills grew black with forms
That huddled and hasted from the crushing crowds
That choked the hidden hollows lying between.
Long dreary hours, all through that horrible night,
The endless millions rolled from out the mouths
Of the black caverns, waves still following waves
Exhaustless, dark, and dreadful, till the dawn
Of a drear day, that day was none, broke white
And sad as a last death-smile on the hills;
And still the hurrying crowds came hastening on,
Millions on millions, hour by hour they came :

And dim and far as the extremest verge
Of the horizon, where the faint blue hills
Melted into the pallor of the heavens,
Wended the fearful throng, and then went down
Into some nether world beyond my ken.
Night came again with torrents of woeful rain,
And winds that whistled through the ghastly gloom;
And still the unending millions came up
Through the black ragged fissures, till the day
Once more came tossing-troubled on the hills,
Dashing white billows of glory in his path,
That turned to pallors of death upon their brows;
And through that day the millions wended on
O'er plain and mountain, out into the east,
Till night dropped down with thunder in her hand,
And forked lightnings played round her zone,
That shot upon the dazeless eyes of all
That ever-gathering multitude, that turned
Their scatheless sockets up to the blue blaze
With melancholy meaning :—On, and on,
For ever and for ever came the crowds,
Till the soul sickened :—On and on,
Millions on millions, crowds on crushing crowds,
For ever and for ever.

                     Till at last,
Just as the day broke with an angry blaze
Over the edges of the mountain peaks,
Out of that black and weltering abyss,

Out of that ghastly death-throng glode, you four—
Thou and thy children—meekly, silently,
With balm and healing, and with calm love-looks;
And straightway all the scene was changed.   I lay
Beneath the quiet boom of summer boughs,
Dallying softly with the teasing winds,
That rippled up among the shadowy leaves—
Still cool with night dews in the early dawn—
And shook down honey and odour.   By my side
Sparkled a tiny river, where I slaked
The feverous thirst that burned within my blood;
And, looking on you all, ye seemed so near,
And yet so strangely far, so true and real,
And yet so evanescent, sweet, and dim—
Wrapped in dream-azures and in mists of sleep—
That, as I stretched my arms to clasp you all,
To fold you to my soothed and softened heart,
Four cloudy shapes passed by me, and I woke,
And heard the sword-blades ringing sharp and near,
And shouts and clamours of victory and defeat,
And all the fury of battle by my tent.

And now I see you all, so like my dreams,
But with no glances in your deep dark eyes
Looking afar; I touch you, and behold!
No cloudy phantom passes through my arms;
I press you to my heart, and do not wake
To wounds and agony, and sounds of war
Jangling dread arms for ever!

                              There they lie,
My innocent babes ! all folded up in sleep
Silent and sweet as flowers ; all their day-smiles
Hanging in rosy hues upon their cheeks,
All their day-laughter lying deep and warm
In silken dimples ; all their daily tasks,
Their garland-gatherings in the empurpled woods,
Forgotten, or enacted o'er in dreams.
How sweet they look !—the two meek infant girls,
Each in her little nest, and the bright boy,
With merry thoughts shut up within the lids
Of his dark dreaming eyes, and laughing out
Of the rich reel of his ambrosial curls.

Oh ! if we could but draw aside the veil
Which hangs between them and futurity,—
Could see the bright and dew-sprent path of youth
All through its many windings, and behold
The poisonous reptiles coiled amid its flowers,
And the grim company of beasts of prey
Lurking amid the thickets by the way,—
Could we behold the far-off ghostly shapes
Poising their poisoned barbs even as we speak,
And waiting in the mists of distant years
For the set time to flame before the eyes
Of their now slumbering victims,—could we see
The man and woman in the sleeping child,
Catch the wan woe-look on the budding cheek,
Hear the thick sighs of sorrow in the dark,

And read the history from this dawning time
When the young steps stumble through clumps of
    flowers,
And the young heart dances its fill of glee,
And the young soul wears all its gala-robes,
On through the distance, till the lone-path winds
Over the craggy heights that cut the feet,
And where, weary and wan, with garments soiled,
And hair dishevelled, through the wind and rain,
With red eyes blinded by the storms o' the world,
They go grief-laden past the hollow caves
Strewn o'er with bones, and stretch their woe-worn
    hands
Out towards the distant arches, lying low
And dim and dark, beyond the mountain-slopes,
Through which the weary walk to endless rest—
With what an agony of love we'd press
The little brows now lying milky white!
We should hear sorrow surging in each tone,
And hollow wails sounding through every laugh,
And every look would catch the haggard hue
Of passing suffering, every word would be
Symbolic of some agony to come,
And every childish antic seem to wave
Some grim old woe out of its cavern-hold ;
And every innocent wile would be the dress
Wherein gaunt wretchedness was quaintly dight,
And every look a window where the face
Of some pale spectre came to sun itself.

But now they live, sweet in the present hour
As untouched roses cool with evening dew,
Reposing on the present, with no fear
Shooting athwart the heaven of their dreams,
And lying beautiful and hushed in sleep
As though each morrow were a festal morn,
And they its chosen actors.

SPRING AND SUMMER.

I.

SPRING.

WITH joy the heart of Earth o'erfills;
　Sun-linked and golden go the hours;
With fainter murmur from the hills
Voluptuously the sleek-tongued rills
　Are lipping honeyed mouths of flowers.

In garden-plots the tulip blows,
　The Bacchanalian peonies burn,
And pansies, in delicious rows,
Make purple glooms, in whose repose
　Their golden hearts like stars outyearn.

Blowing cherry-blooms fall and fall
　Silently, through the silent noon;
Peach-blossoms stain the garden-wall,—
The very air, with the odour of all,
　In a poppied trance doth swim and swoon.

Rich hazes over the orient creep;
   With a softer glory swells the beam;
Trembles of splendour surge and sweep;
In a flood of light the orchards sleep
   Thick bloomed, and gorgeous as a dream.

Like a gold-tipped spear, the high church spire
   Doth gleam and lighten on the view,
With its glowing vane that would aspire
In bickering light, with a tongue of fire,
   To hold high converse with the blue.

Spring in Earth's pulses burns and glows;
   In bursts of music pass her hours;
Her brimming being overflows,
Her life is fragrant as a rose,
   And her deep heart goes out in flowers.

II.

SUMMER.

Lo! lazy Summer, swarthy in the sun,
   Lies panting, with bare breasts, upon the hills,
Swathing her limbs in hazes warm and dun,
Where splendours into dusky splendours run,
   And sultry glory all the heaven o'erfills.

Not a white dimple stirs amid the corn,
　Not a low ripple shivers through the leaves ;—
Since, wrapped in gold and crimson gleams unshorn,
Came, flashing through the east, the regal morn,
　No throated twitterings gurgle round the eaves.

Flooded in sunny silence sleep the kine ;
　In languid murmurs brooklets float and flow ;
The quaint farm-gables in the rich light shine,
And round them jasmined honeysuckles twine,
　And close beside them sun-flowers burn and blow.

Amid the growing heat I lie me down,
　And into visions swarms the moted air ;
Gleams up before me many a famous town,
Pillared and crested with a regal crown
　Outshimmering in an orient purple glare ;

Lo ! lowly Tadmor, burning in its sands—
　Baelbeck and Babylon :—I see slow streams
Gliding by mosque and minaret,—see the gleams
Of seas in sunset—slips of shining strands,
　And drowsy Bagdad buried deep in dreams ;—

See swarthy monarchs flushed in purple rings
　Of silken courtiers ;—through half-open doors
Catch the spice-odours, and the cool of springs
Leaping for ever in a maze of wings,—
　See light forms dancing over pearly floors ;—

Sleeping seraglios, spire, and tremulous dome
   Winking in drowsy splendour all the day,—
See forest haunts where thick the lions roam,—
See thirsty panthers splashed in bloody foam
   Leap terrible as lightnings on their prey;

Or stand with Cortez on a mountain-peak
   Above the Aztec city,—see unrolled
Gem-threaded shores of Montezuma weak,—
See the white temples swarming thick and sleek,
   And sunny streets stretch up by towers of gold;

See silken sails float by, ambrosial,
   Laden with spices, up a Persian glen;
Or stand on Lebanon, 'mid the cedars tall,
Or hear the soft and silver fall
   Of water down a jut of Darien.

But lo! a waking shiver in the trees,
   And voices 'mid the hay-cocks in the glen;
The sun is setting; and the crimson seas
Are shaken into splendour by the breeze,
   And all the busy world is up again!

———oo⊱⊰oo———

REMORSE.

THE stony garlands wreath about the roof,
And up the fluted pillars; snakes of stone
Wind round stone fruits; and clumps of flowers and
    stems,
And pallid leaflets, wrought in marble, start
Out of the chiselled cornices; the stairs
That wind into the distant glooms, where lamps
Golden the far-off gorgeousness, are rich
And jocund with the swarms of slaves
Who wait upon the royal festival;
The halls are all aflame; the tables groan
Under their load of meats, and fruits, and wines;
The guests are all assembled, and the host—
The royal entertainer—sits in state,
His best friend at his side.
              Let the wine wink,
Let mellow laughter gladden o'er the wine,
Let the lamps blaze, let all the lights laugh down
Over the ruddy cheeks of all the fruits,
Let all the costly tables clink with gold,
And let the merriest chant his merriest tale,
Let the stone globes burst out with purple juice,
And the stone serpent trail through crimson flowers,

And the stone stems sprout out their living buds,
And all the ceiling tumble o'er with blooms
In the high-mounting jubilance—and yet
There is a white and glimmering ghastliness
Somewhere behind the arras—ah! and yet
There is a shadow on the royal feast,
And yet—and yet—the wine is not so red
But it hath caught the pallor that is hid
Somewhere behind the arras!

THE TWO GRAVES.

I.

In the lonely twilight,
In the dewy twilight,
　　Lie they softly by each other,
　　　　Hearing not,
　　　　Fearing not—
　　My sister and my mother!
And amid the lonely twilight,
　　Twilight hushed and dim,
Stand I dreaming of a summer
　　And a brooklet's dimpled brim;
And I hear a silver laughter
　　Rippling up the sultry air,
And I see a blithe form dancing
　　In a dusk of darkling hair,
And I feel the cool leaves flout me,
And a storm of flowers about me,
　　Flung forth by that tiny hand;—
Well I know that little dancer
　　On the narrow marge of sand,
And those dimples, and that laughter,
　　And that tiny faëry hand,

And I murmur out "My sister—
　　O my sister!" where I stand;—
But no answer from the twilight,
From the dusk and dewy twilight,
　　Save the moan of far-off waves,—
Nothing but a mourner listening
　　By two green and grassy graves,
Nothing but a single mourner
　　And two green and grassy graves!

II.

In the lonely twilight,
In the dewy twilight,
　　Lie they softly by each other,
　　　　　Hearing not,
　　　　　Fearing not—
My sister and my mother!
And amid the sobbing twilight,
　　Twilight wet and blear,
Stand I dreaming of a winter—
　　Winter icy-stark and drear;
And I lie amid the shadows
　　Of a pallid, noiseless room,
And I see my younger brothers
　　Streaming stormy through the gloom,
And wild eyes are gleaming on me
　　In a lurid thunder-race,
And the wind amid the curtains
　　Dashes horrors in my face,—

Goblin-features dimly seen,
Faces seamed, and gaunt, and lean,
Flickering in a ghastly sheen
   In fever, round my head;
When, behold! a gliding footstep
   Rustles softly towards my bed,
And I feel the milky coolness
   Of a white and loving hand;—
Well I know that gliding footstep,
   And that influence dewy-bland,
And that shower of balmy kisses,
   And the pressure of that hand!
And I stammer out "My mother—
   O my mother!" where I stand;—
But no answer from the twilight,
From the wet and sobbing twilight,
   Save the plash of distant waves,—
Nothing but a mourner weeping
   By two green and silent graves,
Nothing but a single mourner
   And two green and silent graves!

III.

In the lonely twilight,
In the dewy twilight,
   Lie they softly by each other,
              Hearing not,
              Fearing not—
My sister and my mother!

And amid the hovering twilight,
  Twilight of the summer prime,
Stand I dreaming of an evening
  Of the holy olden time ;
And I see two figures kneeling
  In the moonlight of a room,
With their faces leaning upward
  Through the rich and mellow gloom ;
One is listening,—one is praying
  With a heaven-appealing hand ;—
Well I know the low voice speaking
  Of the bright and better land,
And the meek and silent listener,
  And the heaven appealing hand !
And I murmur out "My mother
  And my sister !" where I stand ;—
But no answer from the twilight,
From the hovering summer twilight,
  Save the sob of wakeful waves,—
Nothing but a mourner standing
  By two dim and dusky graves,
Nothing but a single mourner
  And two dim and dusky graves !

IV.

In the lonely twilight,
In the dewy twilight,
  Lie they softly by each other,
                    Hearing not,

Fearing not—
My sister and my mother!
And amid the bleaching twilight,
   Twilight of the crisping rime,
Stand I dreaming of a golden,
   Warbling, flower-flushed summer-time;
And I see a young form gliding
   Down among the shadowy trees,
Faint and languid, in the languor
   Of the odorous summer-breeze,
Faint amid the breathing blossoms,
   And the sultry hum of bees;
And I see her in the evening
   Sinking spent upon her chair,
And I mark the patient tremble
   Of the hand within her hair :—
Comes an angel down unto her
   In the silence of the night,
And he whispers low, " My daughter,
   Forth with me into the light!
Come unto the better country,
   Where they pant no more for breath,—
Past the stark but sleepy terrors
   In the windy halls of Death,—
Down the dark and leaden pathway
   Dug of old by ancient sin.
Lo ! the Master's wedding-garment;
   Thou shalt surely enter in !"
And she takes the wedding-garment

Underneath the solemn stars,
  And the angel at the portal
    Draws aside the gleaming bars,
For behold! her feet have wandered
    Through the windy halls of Death,—
Past the stark and sleepy terrors
    That aye pant and heave for breath,—
Down the dark and leaden pathway
    Dug of old by ancient sin,
And the angel draws the gold bars,
    And she meekly enters in!
But I cannot, cannot see her
    In that glory-streaming land,
Nor the flushing of her features
    As she wanders on the strand,
Nor the flutter of her garments,
    Nor the waving of her hand,
Though I cry aloud—" My sister,
    O my sister!" where I stand ;—
Still no answer from the twilight,
From the bleak and rimy twilight,
    Save the rush of roaring waves,—
Nothing but a mourner shivering
    By two white and frozen graves,
Nothing but a shivering mourner
    And two white and frozen graves !

V.

In the lonely twilight,
In the dewy twilight,
  Lie they softly by each other,
              Hearing not,
              Fearing not—
  My sister and my mother!
And amid the tender twilight,—
  Swimming twilight rich and dim,—
Stand I dreaming of a white face,
  And a whispered midnight hymn;
And I feel an arm about me,
  Pressing with a trembling cling,
And I whisper words of cheering,
  Murmuring of the coming Spring.
And I guide the fainting footsteps
  Gently through the darkened rooms,
And I hear the laboured breathing
  Through the hush of gathering glooms;
Comes the angel down unto her
  With another at his side;
Well I know that milk-white angel,
  With his silent, moonlike slide,
And the garments of the other
  Meek-browed spirit at his side;
Come they shimmering down unto her
  In the silence of the night,
And he whispers low, "My sister,

Forth with us into the light!
Come unto the better country,
　　Where they pant no more for breath,—
Past the blind and trembling terrors
　　In the gusty halls of Death,—
Down the drear and windy pathway
　　Dug of old by ancient sin.
Lo! the Master's wedding-garment;
　　Thou shalt surely enter in!"
And she also takes the garment
　　Underneath the solemn stars,
And the angel at the portal
　　Draws aside the gleaming bars;
For, behold! she too has wandered
　　Through the gusty halls of Death,
Past the blind and trembling terrors
　　That for ever gasp for breath,
Down the steep and windy pathway
　　Dug of old by ancient sin,
And the angel draws the gold-bars,
　　And she also enters in!
But I cannot hear their greetings
　　As they touch the shining strand,
For they render back no token
　　From the bright and better land—
Not the whimple of a garment,
　　Not the waving of a hand,
Though I moan aloud,—"My sister
　　And my mother!" where I stand—

Comes no answer from the twilight,
From the trembling, dewy twilight,
　　Save the gentle fall of waves,
Nothing but a mourner dreaming
　　By two soft and silent graves,
Nothing but a dreaming mourner
　　And two soft and silent graves!

VI.

In the deeper twilight,
In the later twilight,
　　Lie they softly by each other,
　　　　　Hearing not,
　　　　　Fearing not—
My sister and my mother!
And amid the deeper twilight,
　　Twilight hushed and steeped in dew,
Stand I dreaming of this old world,
　　And the ever-budding new,—
Of the many base and selfish,
　　And the bright and blessed few;
With strange visions, broken, starry,
　　Of the regions hid from view,
Glimpses of the golden splendours
　　Peopled with angelic wings,
Glistening glades, and sliding rivers,
　　Forest-haunts of milk-cool springs,
Faces moonlike with the gladness
　　Caught from looking unto HIM,

Golden waves of music rushing
  From rapt lyres of seraphim,
Billows of ecstatic worship,
  Garments in their purple splendour
  Many-folded, rolling dim,
Sparry glistenings from the gateways,
  Glinting glories from the street,
And the ever-dimpling music
  Of the white and dewy feet;
Then, of all the dreary future
  Looming through the misty years,
Cheerless toil and thankless labour,
  And the bitter cup of tears;
And I murmur, "Would, ye bright ones!
  That this stormy race was o'er,
That my barque might drift up lightly
  To your silver-rippled shore,
That this weary, weary struggle,
  And this sordid strife were o'er,
That my life might float out softly
  To your boundless evermore,
That the Master's wedding-garment
  I might also safely win,
For alas! the world is weary,
  And I too would enter in!"
When, behold! the tender moonlight
  Swimming o'er the slumbering land,
And amid the floating splendour
  Breathes a blessing holy, bland;

Sliding down the silken star-stairs
   From the bright and better land,
And a peace is in the murmured
   "Mother, sister," where I stand;
Though no voice is in the moonlight,
In the sleek and sleepy moonlight,
   Save the silver fall of waves,
Nothing but a silent mourner
   By two deep and tender graves,
Yet a holier-hearted mourner
   By two deep and tender graves,
Yes! a holier-hearted mourner,
   And two deep and tender graves!

AN INDIAN SUNSET.

———

THROUGH the verandah came the laden winds
With spices and the breath of odorous gums.
The west was all aflush with the rich hues—
Azure and crimson, swart and sanguine gold,
And bickering saffron, as the day went down.
All the trees swam in sunset; all the boughs
Shook in swift spasms of fire, as every breath
Swept the balms off them; every copse and brake
Lay laden with the sweets of summer time;
And out from all the heats the evening came
Dispensing the cool blessing of the dews,
And gathering up into her dripping skirts
The fiery seeds of morrows yet to come.

Like lightning in his cloud, the panther slept,
With all his spots reposing on their gold,
Save when some footstep of the coming night
Sent dusky shiverings down his tawny sides,
And sudden gleams of expectation to his eyes.
The lion slumbered in his leafy lair;
The tiger licked his paws; and the red eyes
Of the yet drowsy wolf just gleamed and broke
In lurid flashes on the deepening dusk.

Swooning with joy the sultry day down sank,
In gleaming hues of crimson—glory robes,
Shot through with streaks of purple and fine gold;
The heavens surged with saffron, with still depths
Of slowly-darkening amethyst, o'er which
Fell subtle flakes of fire, and floating pomps
Of ruddy clouds went by, and, dim with light,
Were banks with nebulous shores, within whose
    bounds
Bright skiffs of wondrous splendour swept the heavens,
And spirits of mist leapt out in light, like gods.

And so the daily miracle went on :
The Sun built himself cities in the heavens,
And heaped them o'er with riches, pile on pile,
Pillar on pillar, street on flaming street,
Huge rolling domes, and pinnacles of gold,
Long corridors of far-retreating deeps ;
Then, weary with his work, he seized his wand,
And at the magic touch the tottering towers,
Fretworks of silver, gleaming gates of gold,
Pillars, and rounded roofs, and shafts of light,
Tumbled in gorgeous ruin ; till the prone
And squandered splendours, at his will supreme,
Turned into life fantastic, changed their shape,
And all the loosened glories burned and glowed,
Rolled into hills of gems, and craggy heights
Of purest amber ; floated ships ablaze
Sailing down seas of purple ; writhed like snakes

Suddenly caught within a forest of fire ;
Bulged into argosies of gleaming wealth ;—
Down the day sank ; and all the glories went
In sullen lapsings of splendour, ebb by ebb,
Purple by purple, pomp by crowding pomp,
Till leaden windings of Lethe-streams, and swamps
Of gloom grew greening on the dusky verge
Of the on-coming darkness—on, and on,
Till Night came, like a stern dark Fate,
And brushed the busy pageantry away.

THE HERO'S WIDOW.

———

HE clomb the heights of danger
    To deathless fame, they said,—
The bullets hurtling round him,
    The banner o'er his head,
Defiance in his wild shout,
    Jove's thunder in his hand,
And in his eye the lightning
    That bickered o'er his brand!
With his plume i' the bellowing tempest
    High tossing o'er the rest;
And where War's lance was keenest
    His breast the foremost breast,
And where the cannon shouted
    Fire-tongued in their own might,—
Where'er the fight was deadliest
    He deadliest in the fight!
For he fought for holy freedom
    And England's old renown,
And where he stood a victor
    He found a martyr's crown!

        I only know, she answered,
            He is not at my side;

My breast is not his pillow,
  I am no more his bride.
Red War's loud roar still thunders,
  But it does not pale my brow;—
I have ceased my prayer—*He* is not there,
  I do not tremble now!

Amid the clash and clangour
  Where reddest ran the flood,
Where swords were wildly leaping
  To the hilt in foemen's blood,
Where the storm of plumes was thickest,
  And the bayonets hid the sun,
Where the rattling shots leapt out in fire
  From many a smoking gun,
Where the legions swung like billows
  On a mad and tossing sea,
And the tug and strife for right and life
  Swelled high war's anarchy;
Amid the murky darkness
  He burst like a shock of flame,—
His name shall aye be deathless
  Who went through death to fame!
For he fought for holy freedom
  And England's old renown,
And where he stood a victor
  He found a martyr's crown!

  I only know, she answered,
    He is not at my side;

My breast is not his pillow,
  I am no more his bride.
Red War's loud roar still thunders,
  But it does not pale my brow ;—
I have ceased my prayer—*He* is not there,
  I do not tremble now !

THE SAME AND NOT THE SAME.

THE summer sunshine played upon our path,
The summer sunshine, and the warm south wind;
And from the billowy hill-top, where we stood,
We watched the lazy ships glide out to sea,
Past the green island and its ruined church,
That slept in peace amid the pleasant trees
Down-bending in low, whispering lullabies.
The green sweet island, with its hoary fane
And drowsy, humming trees, that o'er the sea,
Just dimpled into silver by the breeze,
Cast a long, cooling shadow:—Ah! that noon,
Filled with the buzz and boom of happy wings
Wheeling amid the sunshine on our path,
The summer sunshine, and the warm south wind!

Far down below us, on the white, hot road
Some boys were pulling apples from the boughs,
Merry as wreathed and dancing Bacchanals,
Their shouts of laughter running up the hill
In honeyed ripples, 'mong the heather-bells;
And, midway up the mountain, an old man
Crawled like a beetle in the shining day;

While on the left a low-browed cottage stood
Full in the sunshine of that golden noon,
With its old yew-tree by the ivied porch
Holding a dusky coolness in its boughs,
And making pleasant murmurs to the bees;
And a young girl upon the breezy slope
Was playing on the greensward with a lamb,
Now frisking with it in the crisping grass,
And now down lying underneath a tree
Twining a wreath of mosses round its neck
In laughter-dimpled gladness!—Ah! that noon,
Filled with the buzz and boom of happy wings
Wheeling amid the sunshine on our path,
The summer sunshine, and the warm south wind!

Down on our right, the sunny town lay still,
Just folded in a thin, white haze of smoke,
Its sleepy clock low-tolling out the hour;
The sluggish, heated town, thick with sun-motes,
Low lying mid the dim and shadowy fields
With all their tawny wealth of ripening corn;
And round about us hummed the golden bees
Heavy with honey from the tulip-plots,
And peaches warm i' the sun, and mellowing pears;
And butterflies came fluttering their warm wings,
Purple and crimson, dusk and sultry gold;
And dragon-flies went gleaming through the air,
Gorgeous as Juno and her peacock steeds;
And all the glory of that carnival time

Lay like a slumber on the happy earth
In her glad, teeming plenty ;—when, behold !
Mighty as Mars—Bellona at his side
In all the terror of her sounding thongs,
Smiting the silence backward to the hills,
Rushed the long thundering train ;—a glory plume
Melting in sunshine followed at its wake—
Past the still grange, and slumbering rookery,
Startling the milk-kine sleeping on the slope,
On through the valley with its silent farms,
And the warm languor of the whitening corn ;
On through the sunny distance, till the noon,
Drowsy though humming, sank again in sleep,
And we could hear the waggons, down below,
Rolling, hay-laden, through the deep, white lanes,
And heard the creaking barn-door swinging wide,
And murmured hum of voices :—Ah ! that noon,
Filled with the buzz and boom of happy wings
Wheeling amid the sunshine on our path,
The summer sunshine, and the warm south wind !

Now, as I stand upon the howling hill,
A scene of desolation lies below,
Wild as a lone moor, with its single tarn
And drowned girl floating through the slobbering
        waste,
Her dead eyes open to the windy rain !
No boys are pulling apples from the trees
That make an iron music to the blast,

Tossing their bare boughs in the wintry wind,
Gaunt as worn maniacs shrivelled to the bone.
The little girl has vanished from the slope,
Her voice is hushed, and the pet lamb is dead.
The sunshine has abandoned the stark world,
The birds are shivering in the dripping boughs,
The imploring winds seek rest and find it not,
Sending shrill wails above the cold, drowned
    earth.

Now, as I stand upon the howling hill,
The sea flings its salt spray about the church:
I see the white waves through the slanting rain,
Leaping in fury round the dreary isle,
But cannot hear their roaring for the wind.
The tumbled sea-gulls, blown about the sky,
Strive to win inland from the frenzied shore;
The desolate farms loom dimly through the rain,
Each standing stagnant in its separate swamp;
The starveling hedges drip into the pools;
The town is hidden in a swirl of sleet:
I hear the engine shrieking up the wind,
But cannot see it for the blinding rain.
Below me, on the lush and plashing path,
An old bent woman is abroad to-day—
The cold drops drizzling from her flouting rags—
Fighting with wind and tempest for her bread.
She seeks the low-browed cottage on the hill;
She will find winter on its cheerless hearth—

Winter sole inmate of its reeking walls,
And thin winds wailing in its desolate rooms !

My way lies through the churchyard where *she* sleeps—
She who was with me on that sunny noon—
Sleeps?   Aye! though the lean and hungry winds
Are howling, like starved wolves, along the grass,
And though the tempest, in the dripping yews,
Loosens a deluge down upon the graves !

HERE AND THERE.

———

Oh! the July winds were blowing,
And the Avon, full and flowing,
Washed the oak-roots, warm, and growing
      Thick and bent;
Oh! the July winds were blowing
        Warmly blowing,
    When he went!
And I flung my arms around him,
      And he blest me;
And I flung my trembling arms around him,
      And he blest me;
And I begged him in the strife
To beware of his rich life,
And he murmured out, "Sweet wife!"
      And blest me!
(But oh! for the cold, cold rain—
  The rain, and the winds that blow;
The cold, cold rain, and the colder wind—
  The wind, and the rain, and the snow!)

Oh! the blithesome larks were singing,
Full throats were richly flinging

Their hearts down dim woods ringing
      All unspent;
Oh, the blithesome larks were singing,
      Sweetly singing,
    When he went!
And I shook my hair about him,
      And he kissed me;
And I wildly shook my hair about him,
      And he kissed me;
And I told him if he died
I should creep unto his side,
And he murmured out, " Sweet bride!"
      And kissed me!
(But oh! for the cold, cold rain,—
  The rain, and the winds that blow;
The cold, cold rain, and the colder wind—
  The wind, and the rain, and the snow!)

Oh! the humble bees were booming
Where the wild-briar's pearls were looming
In a dusk of branches blooming
      Dew besprent;
Oh! the humble-bees were booming,
      Sweetly booming
    When he went!
And I pressed him to my bosom,
      And he blest me;
And I madly pressed him to my bosom,
      And he blest me;

And I said, if from that shore
He should come to me no more,
When the cruel war was o'er?
   And he blest me!
(But oh! for the cold, cold rain—
 The rain, and the winds that blow;
The cold, cold rain, and the colder wind—
 The wind, and the rain, and the snow!)

Oh! the setting sun was beaming,
And a gorgeous glow was streaming
Over copse and meadow, gleaming
   Glory blent;
Oh! the setting sun was beaming,
   Brightly beaming
When he went!
And I fondly hovered o'er him,
  And he kissed me;
And I fondly, fondly hovered o'er him,
  And he kissed me;
And I said, if in that fight
He should vanish from my sight,
Like a meteor in the night?
   And he kissed me!
(But oh! for the cold, cold rain—
 The rain, and the winds that blow;
The cold, cold rain, and the colder wind—
 The wind, and the rain, and the snow!)

Oh! the eve to night was turning,
And the early stars were yearning
Through a mist of odours, burning,
  Glory blent;
Oh! the eve to night was turning,
   Gently turning,
  When he went!
And with shut eyes clung I to him,
  And he left me!
And with tearful shut eyes clung I to him,
  And he left me!
And with passionate arms I prest him,
And with shuddering spasms I blest him,
And in frenzied haste caressed him,
  And he left me!
(But oh! for the cold, cold rain—
 The rain, and the winds that blow;
The cold, cold rain, and the colder wind—
 The wind, and the rain, and the snow!)

ODE ON THE BIRTH OF BURNS.*

I.

A HUNDRED times, with clangorous shout and din,
Have tower and steeple hailed the New Year in;
A myriad brazen throats, a hundred times,
Have wildly chanted forth their Christmas chimes;
A hundred times the ancient world hath rolled
Out of the lap of summer, warm with gold,
Into the bleaching wind and drenching rain,
Since first the wondrous peasant felt the air,
Since first above his head a mother's prayer
Went fluttering up to God, amid the angelic train.

II.

No royal palace was prepared for him;
No silent courtiers slid from room to room,
Gathering together in the gorgeous gloom
Of purple hangings, drooping rich and dim;
For him no silver cressets shed their light,
No eager joy-bells sounded through the night
From city minster, or from village tower,
No loud hurrahs, sent from deep-chested men

---

* One of the six recommended to be published by the judges of
the Crystal Palace Competition, on the centenary of the birth of
Robert Burns.

Lifted the midnight mist from off the glen
In celebration of his natal hour ;
No hush of deep expectance filled the earth ;
No cry rose rich with gladness at his birth ;
The noble revelled at his sumptuous hall ;
The beauty bloomed and languished at the ball ;
The drowsy miller scolded at the mill ;
The peasant slept beneath the misty hill ;
The heavens were still ; no shaggy lightnings came
To burn the midnight in their eager ire ;
No mighty portent, with a pen of fire,
Scribbled upon the dark the poet's name ;
He came and no man knew it ; no man knew
The wondrous boon to Scotland given ;
That there—beneath that grim and wintry blue—
A glorious poet, strong and true,
Had newly dropped from heaven !

III.

Nature herself lay still, and dumb, and cold ;
Gone were her summer garments fringed with gold,
Her gorgeous sunsets, streaked with crimson bars—
Darkling in violet depths, shot through with light—
Deepening in splendour as the enchantress, Night,
Gathered and creamed the dim light into stars ;
Gone were her balms and blooms, her hum of bees,
Her sweet-mouthed zephyrs toying with the trees,
Her honeyed murmurings under hedge-rows dim,

Where happy lovers spent their evening hours,
Her festival array of cups and flowers,
Full of rich nectar to the fiery brim ;
Gone was the banquet and the golden sheen,
The lights were out, the revelry was o'er,
And she who, erstwhile, was a crownèd queen,
Shivered a beggar at her palace-door.
Giving scant welcome to the new-born child,
She seized him in her stiff arms, lank and cold,
And held him out upon the wintry wold,
To look upon the desolation, strange and wild,
Which weirdly shuddered down on farm and fold,
In rain, and sleet, and silent-falling snow—
Wrapping the heavens in a pall above,
And the dead earth in a white shroud below.

IV.

A wintry path, a future thick with gloom,
Solid as adamant, before him lay,
Through which the poet cleft his lonely way,
'Mid menace and reproach and muttering doom,
Into the dawning of that better day
Which now has settled down upon his tomb.
For nature hath a Spartan mother's heart,
And, to prepare her noblest for their part
In the stern strife and struggle, she ordains
Rude tasks, hard fare, and bitter cups of pains—
Knowing the heroic stature is built higher

By toil and suffering, and the hero shows
Kingliest and grandest when his forehead glows
Beneath that burning zone—the martyr's crown of
　　fire.

V.

And so he grew and wrestled for the right;
True man! true bard! who battled with the strong;
And, having crowned his poverty with song,
He brought it boldly forth into the light,
Heedless of jibe or jeer; and all men sought
To see the wonder which the bard had wrought;
Great, as though under some enchanter's rod,
A shapeless block of stone had shimmered out a god!

VI.

He took his country to his inmost soul,
And sang her joys and sorrows as his own;
And in his verse we hear her wild winds moan,
The rapid rustle of her brooks, and roll
Of her rude rivers, as they dash and foam
In tawny fury round the shepherd's home.
Her Doric speech, her heart of simple truth,
Her piety and strength, her tales of ruth,
Her fireside legends, and her wild romance
Glitter and gather in a rustic dance,
Laughing in garlands of perpetual youth,

Within the magic circle of his rhymes;
And Scottish faëries ring their silver chimes,
Goblin and ghost, warlock and witch uncouth,
And all the marvels of the olden times
Troop forth at his behest;
And every terror of his native land
Shakes out its elf-locks, bares its bony hand,
And every sportive whim, at his command,
Sits down the poet's guest.

VII.

Laughter and tears alike were at his nod,
Humour and wit ran sparkling rich as wine;
And at the rare carousal, half divine,
He sat amid his subjects, like a god
Waited upon by satyrs.
                               Like a bee,
He sipped sweet honey from the bitterest flower;
And at his touch the starkest wintry tree
Rained down its apples in a golden shower.
Young men and maidens whisp'ring, still rehearse
Their joys and sorrows in his manly verse;
His witching words still well o'er budding lips,
Mantling soft cheeks in ruddy dimple-dips
And innocent laughters of the ancient prime;
And still, at hearthstone, and at rural fair,
Old men and matrons, heeding not that Time

Hath furrow'd cheek and brow, and blanch'd the
    glossy hair,
Chuckle and murmur o'er the magic rhyme,
Brimful of life and light, and all youth's dainty fare;
Nature, full-lipped, was singing in his heart;
And, though the wounded poet felt the smart
Of poverty, yet, like a bird in spring,
Soul-full of music, he did nought but sing,
And in the choral whole, he grandly bore his part.

BIRTH-DAY STANZAS.

TO ———

ON HIS ATTAINING HIS TWENTY-FIRST BIRTH-DAY.

OVER all the greening valleys
    Breathes the dewy balm of spring,
Over all the shadowy woodlands
    Burst the notes of welcoming;
And a brighter light is streaming
    Over all the world to-day,
For it is the gleesome spring-tide,
    'Tis the merry month of May!

With a gladder note the skylark
    Flutters up to meet the morn,
With a richer note the black-bird
    Warbles from the tufted thorn,
With a softer voice the streamlet
    Lisps its whispered love-song gay,
For it is the happy spring-tide,
    'Tis the merry month of May!

And a dawn of gorgeous promise
    Trembles over wood and wold,

Waiting for the regal Summer
  And her pomp of green and gold ;
Waiting for the full fruition
  Of the blossoms of to-day,
Oh ! it is the happy spring-time,
  'Tis the merry month of May !

So, my friend, may your spring morning
  Scatter fragrant promise round ;
So, with trophy-wreaths and garlands,
  May your after years be crown'd ;
May a rich and sumptuous summer
  Of good deeds begin to-day,
May the God of heaven be with you
  In your merry, merry May !

THE ISLAND PRINCE.

DREAM FRAGMENTS.

Up from his crimson cushions and his couch
Broidered with gold the King rose wearily.
He flung aside his purples, and went out
Into the humming woods. Nor heeded he
The lotus in the water, nor the shine
And startled splendour of the birds that glanced
Through cinnamon groves, and boughs of orange
      trees,
Nor all the fruits that dangled in his way,
Sun-ripe to the very core; nor the dim cloud
Of blended incense, that, at every step,
Rose up from all the rich empurpled banks.
He passed a festal party, who, with cheeks
Glowing with health, and eyes that gleamed with
      glee,
Danced to the clash of cymbals, heedlessly,
And plunged into the thicker forest glooms.
His heart sang of the past; and as that lake
Whose outer verge reflects Potosi's towers
And blazing domes, all dimpled into gold,
But whose secreted waters, subterrene,

Preserve unrotting whatso'er they hold,
And sometimes, breaking through the golden bars
Wherein Peruvian miners hold them bound,
Disgorge their treasures from their caverned deeps,—
Their hoarded dead of many centuries,
With the rude bloom of health fixed on their cheeks,
No dimple worn away, no hair displaced,
Arrayed in all the quaint dress of the past,
And dancing suddenly sunned upon the waves,
Known from the living only by their garb,—
Even so his soul swarmed thick with other years,
That came up to the surface, long entombed,
Yet all undimmed and lustrous as this hour;—
Came with their parted hair, and smiling lips,
And meek-clasped hands, and moveless feet, and felt
The sun upon their white and pulseless brows.
Onward he plunged, until he reached a spot
Where the o'er-hanging branches wreathed above
A dim grot lying low, and cool, and green,
Wherein a rivulet darted darkly-bright
O'er tawny pebbles, and embrownèd sand,
And shells with lips that curled from pearl to pink.
Here, couched on yielding mosses, down he sank,
Till all his fancy into visions broke:
Chiefly of England, and the golden prime
Of Chivalry in the bright-plumèd past,
Tales told him in the sumptuous autumn nights,
Dropping with honey, by famed travellers.
He saw the stormy Viking ride the waves;

He heard the burly baron clang his steel;
He saw the beard of Merlin waving white;
And all the pageantry of Arthur's court
At joust and tournament. The mighty brand
Durandal, flashes all its magic light
Full in his face; he sees Astolpho's lance
Divide the darkness of the meeting boughs;
Sir Guy of Warwick, Lancelot of the Lake,
Sir Roland, and the Cid go by all plumed,
Jingling their golden trappings. He beholds
The towers of fabled Camelot, and sees
The silken ladies glancing up the streets;
Enchanted palaces, with blazing fronts,
Yearning towards the south, within whose rooms,
Guarded by griffins, lo! the Princess lies;
And hoary castles swarm above the woods,
Their wondrous towers all tumbling into mist,
Reeling in flame and sunset o'er his eyes.
A sleep seals all his senses; down he goes
A laden pilgrim through the world of dreams.

'Tis broad mid-day. The hunt is done. The horns,
Far off, sound the recall. He is alone.
The forest shimmers o'er him; and a sense
Of being here by some foredoomed appointment
Weighs heavy on his soul; some great event
Seems summoning its thunders in the heavens
To herald its approach. Faint on the air
The echo of the horns dies far away,

And all the world of men, and busy deeds
Falls from him in his trance ; he is alone.
When lo ! a wonder wrought before his eyes ;
Some unseen power catches the forest up,
And all the mighty trunks and twisted boughs
Writhe groaning as in fire, and disappear
Utterly, leaving not a cloud or speck
On the gold disc of day.   On he is urged
By some invisible hand, until he sees
Broadening before his steps, a valley wide,
Fragrant with spices of the sunny south,
And musical with voices of the spring,
Stretch up into the crimson-clouded east,
Where in a purple mist, a city glowed,
With gorgeous domes, and winking cupolas,
And golden spires, that in the mellow light
Shot out bewildering lances of keen fire.

In sooth a pleasant valley ! full of brooks,
And the low murmurs of the well-pleased winds,
And voices rich with gladness, and sweet bursts
Of tremulous music sent from carolling hearts ;—
A valley dark with dim voluptuous fruits,
And flowers that shook upon their fragrant stems,
And groves of spices bleeding odorous gums ;—
But on the one side, hung a forest hoar
With tossing boughs, and branches bleak and bare,
Through whose dark solitudes went wailing winds,
And sounds of dolour, and dim shapes of woe ;—

And on the other rose, with ragged peaks,
A tumbled world of grey and cruel rocks;
And mid the flowers of the valley gleamed
The deadly beauty of the gliding snake,
And, mingled with the fruits, were poisonous shrubs
That hung their crimson globes amid the vines.

On towards the shining city in the east,
Two forms were wending on the valley-path.
The one was human; but the other shone
With a meek lustre, as the harvest moon
After still rain, upon a breathless night
Hangs low and large above the dripping boughs;
And where she passed, a richer fragrance breathed
From out the cool hearts of the dewy flowers,
And to the clustering fruits, a mellower hue
Ran o'er the tan of their suffusèd cheeks;
While all the poisonous berries shrivelled up
Their shining purples to the blackened core,
And all the slimy reptiles sought their holes.

At length they reached the city; and the gate
Rolled back in muffled music on its hinge;
And a delicious clamour of loud harps
Stirred all the air to rapture, and a shout,
"Blessed for ever!" ran along the streets,
Through the long length of shining colonnades,
And stately squares and jasper cornices,
And by the golden domes and twinkling spires,—

I

All through the pillared splendour of the place
"Blessed for ever!" rang in jubilant tones;
And then the great gate rolled back on its hinge,
And music welled out o'er the city walls.
Again the vision changes; and behold!
Deep in the centre of the hoary woods,
Where never to the sound of timbrel danced
The swarthy maidens of his native land:
Where never human foot had pressed the grass;
Nor wild beast wandered in the quest of prey:
Where preternatural silence kept a hush
Of centuries, the trees drew back, and left
A space ringed round by broken, moss-grown
  walls:
Where basked no lizard, and no creeping thing
Went in and out the fissures; o'er the gate,
That stood wide open in the moonèd calm
And shadowy glamour of this silent place,
Carved in white marble, white as Polar snows,
Each tender finger trembling in the light,
All soft as water-lilies, was a hand—
A delicate lady's hand—that pointed still
Towards the old house, which, with its high-peaked
  roof,
And many gables, in the garden stood
White in the moonlight. Through the arch he passed,
And stepped upon the lawn, where, high in air,
A fountain played, whose feathery waters fell
Silent as shadows on the pleachèd grass,

And then wound out, through roots of flowering
    shrubs,
And down dim alleys where the starlight shone
Still and transparent, on its breast, as still,
Into some unseen basin far away.
Close by the fountain, on a pillar of brass,
Thrown back, up to the pitiless heavens, a face
Flecked o'er with shadows smote upon his eyes,
And thrilled his soul with horror. On a neck
No thicker than the poisonous cobra gleamed
This ghastly copper phantom:—Oh! a face
Where eld unsearchable, and hate, and scorn,
And agony, were scorched in lava-lines.
The salted fires of preternatural woe
Had washed those thin cheeks ere the Pharaohs went
Clad in asbestos to the mummied ranks
Of their forefathers. On that woman's brow,
Thick-seamed with wrinkles, blazing centuries
Had burned like bars; those dim and sunken eyes
Sought out the blue depths far beyond the moon,
Beyond the stars! beyond the universe,
With savage hate; and from those cruel lips,
Drawn up in untold agony, a cry
Of scorn, and curses, and of countless woes
Seemed ever bursting forth in blistering fire,
But came not, fixed for ever!
                On he passed,
Sickened with dread, urged forward by his dream,
Through an old Gothic doorway, ribbed and rich

With tracery, into a dim-lighted hall,
Where, from the rusted armour on the wall,
Cobwebs hung stirless in the breathless hush,
And moveless shadows clung along the roof,
Save at the upper end, where, like two wings
In some infernal air, two banners black,
With motion slow and regular, flapped all
The horror of that ghastly face, picked out
In sweltering gold, upon the inner gloom.

Onward, from room to room, from door to door,
He passed with tottering knees; and in each room,
Out from some corner, o'er the painted door,
Or grinning down from the deep-groinèd-roof,
Chiselled in stone, or worked in glinting bronze,
Flamed the same hideous face before his eyes.
He ran; he strove to cry; but not a sound
Broke on the peopled stillness of the place.
Onward he darted; and his footsteps fell
Silent as feather-down from molting birds,—
From room to haunted room, striving in vain
To escape the ghastly whirl that, close behind,
Filled all the gloom with faces.   On, and on,
Flying in agony, he dashed the doors
Behind him, to shut out the shapes he knew
Were coming in pursuit—up through the silence—
Up through the dark that drew close on his heels—
And, evermore, he found the pictured walls
Grow still more ghastly; evermore the face

Shuddered out more distinctly from the gloom;
The lank, thin hair almost began to move
On the long serpent neck; the dreadful eyes
Almost began to gleam; and through the lips
The long-pent cry seemed just about to break
In cataracts of curses:

　　　　　　When, behold!
As he smote in a cedar door, and burst
Into the last room of the ghostly range,
A silken couch, beside a window wide
Lay saintly sweet in moonlight; and no more,
Either from doorway, or from painted roof,
Or ghastly-gleaming wall, looked out the face;
But on the couch a veiled form lay in sleep,
Lifting with gentle rise and fall, the silks
That warm and white lay on her breathing breast.
Behold a hand most exquisitely fair—
Twin lily of the one that met his eyes
Brightening the outer arch—and, nestling deep
In gauze, an arm lay on the coverlet,
Daintily rounded as the milky stem
Of flowering balsams. Up he deftly stole,
And, with expectant hand, drew gently back
The veil of samite from the sleeping face:—
Horror of horrors! There, oh! there, at last,
The living hair winds round the serpent-neck;
The living eyes wink up their witcheries
Dead into his! The seamed and ghastly brow,
Like heated brass, is pressed against his own!

There is the ante-type, the living face—
The face of dateless eld—of agony—
Of hate and scorn—is there; and there, hark! hark!
Oh there, at last, the cry!

                        Up from the grass,
The big drops starting on his clammy brow,
The King leapt, startled from his ghastly dream.
The day was done; the stars were high in heaven;
And close beside the bank whereon he slept,
A stealthy step glode through the hush of night,
And not a sound disturbed the dreaming boughs.

URBAN THE MONK.

A German Legend.

PART I.

THE LIBRARY.

I.

Young Urban keeps the burnished keys
Of the Scriptorium; and he sits
Through sunny noons in dreamful ease,
Reading or copying, by fits;
Or adding quaint and golden tints,
Or plushy purples to the page
Of mass-book, or of breviary,
Of holy father, bard, or sage;
Till all the full-lored vellums swim
In crimsons and in purples dim,
And common words, in soft array,
Prance down the page, like palfry gay,
Trapped all in gold, to bear away
The faëry form of princess prim.
And whether round the abbey blow
The soft south winds, with overflow

Of balm and honey, or the snow
Lies white upon the ground below,
And tempests round the belfry go,
'Tis all the same to him !

II.

All through the sunny summer noon,
When lilies over wall-flowers swoon,
And, in the honeyed heart of June,
    The bee on roses feeds—
He pores, amid the shadiest nooks,
Over the gold-illumined books,
With earnest face, and eager looks,
    Believing all he reads.

III.

Legends of saints fill up the gloom
Of winter nights, and drizzling days :—
He sees them swim along his room,
And then wind upward, in a bloom
Of roseate colours, dipt in gloom,
    Wrapped in a trembling haze
Of cloudy splendour, bulging low ;
Billows of fire, as white as snow,
Roll with pale crimsons down below
Their sandal'd feet, with motion slow ;
And round about their bare heads go
    Halos, like sunset rays !

IV.

Of holy martyrs, too, he reads—
Of blessed Blandina—Appian—
Quinta the pure—and Ulpian—
Metra—and blameless Adrian;
Until his young heart pants and bleeds
For those who, for the true faith died;
How some were torn by wild-beasts; some
Flung into boiling pitch; and some
Tormented in the murderous hum
Of Rome, were crucified;
How mangled Porphyry dauntless stood,
With flayed ribs slowly dripping blood,
Daring the tyrant's ire;
How Polycarp, with garments riven,
Went with a holy shout to heaven
On flickering wings of fire!

V.

Mingled with these were legends old
Of wondrous knights and ladies gay;
The Cid, Sir Roland, Tristram bold,
Streamed in rich trappings, jingling gold,
Over the crimson sunset wold,
Adown the sinking day;
And ladies, with a silken swim,
Fluttered along the mossy brim
Of meres, by deep woods hushed and dim,
On to the bright tournáy,

VI.

But chief he loved the mystic story
Of saintly knights, with faces pale,
Who spurned the earth, and earthly glory,
And went in quest of Holy Grail.
He followed them on by land and flood—
Sir Parzival—brave and holy knight—
And bold Sir Galahad—the good;
He heard them clanging through the night,
Over the pavements, still and white,
Their studded bridles jingling light,
Flashing amid the soft moonlight,
And saw them skim along the wood—
Up alleys of moonbeams, trembling pale—
Past church, and city, and lordly tower,
And valley, and swamp, and lady's bower,
All in the hush of the midnight hour,
In quest of Holy Grail!

VII.

Titurel's temple o'er him rose,
Blushing with gems, and gorgeous glows
Of golden domes, and twinkling spires;
Roses of rubies, and pale fires
Of clustered diamonds shook about
The wondrous fabric in and out;
And in the central sanctuary,
On a thick slab of porphyry,

Wrapped in white samite, stood the Grail,
Outshimmering like a cloudy moon;
And o'er it swelled a mimic noon
Of topaz, and of jasper bright,
Hung in the sapphire ceiling light;
Outside, the dome bulged up red gold,
With blue enamel fretted o'er;
And banners, with unruffled fold,
Hung silken out at every door;
And round about the Holy Grail
Rose two-and-seventy chapels, pale
With gold and diamonds; every two
Shot up a tower into the blue
Like sudden flame; and over those
Shook crystal crosses in the light,
Clutched from above within the claws
Of gold spread-eagles, day and night;
And o'er the central dome there rose
A huge carbuncle, with red glows
And sullen splendour, like a sun
Lighting the cypress-forest dun,
That round about the temple stood,
Filling its shadowy heart with blood:—
And none might tread that mystic hight
Of hushed Montsalvage, save the knight
Chosen of Him of holy-rood!

VIII.

And still he turns the gilded leaves ;
And, rich in faith, the monk believes
Further than logic ere hath got :—
His creed soars higher˙than his sight —
Reason is not his only light ;—
Still through the hot bewildered night,
Angels go heavenward, clad in white,
And so he reads, and doubteth not !

~~~~~~~~~~~~~~~~~~~~

PART II.

—

DOUBTING CASTLE.

I.

Alas the day !   Alas the hour !
The sullen clouds, with downward roll,
And heart of hidden thunders lower
Over the brightness of his soul.
He sits in sadness, in his room,
Wrapped in the old Tartarean gloom,
Murmuring, in dire perplexity,
"This is a fearful mystery ;—
I cannot think how this can be !"

II.

It is the holy Sabbath day ;
The Bible rests upon his knee ;

He cannot read, he cannot pray,
Although his lips the words may say
With shuddering effort, yet the "Nay"
Is in his heart; and piteously
He murmurs low—"A mystery—
1 cannot think how this may be!"

III.

Ye pitying heavens help him now!
And take the cloud from off his brow,
And draw the fang from out his smart:—
Into the garden of his heart
The storm hath gone, with cruel cry,
And all is dead from sward to sky!

IV.

For he has read how, unto Him
Who ruleth all things with a nod,
Time is as nought; how unto God
A thousand years are as a day,
Or as a night-watch; and he feels
His heart rock in the stormy "Nay!"
That *will* be heard, both night and day,
Although he struggles hard to pray
And cannot, though he kneels!

V.

At church, he seems a guilty thing;
He hears the full-choired anthems ring

K

With roll, and surge, and golden swing,
The bannered aisles about;
But they have lost the air divine:—
Seems all a blank, and idiot sign,
The bright soul shaken out!

VI.

Through the east window shines the sun,
With mellow splendour, warm and dun;
Through violet tints, and gorgeous streams
Of falling robes, and softest creams
Of rapt saints' halos—flashing gleams
Of roses dankling—mingled beams
Rich as the silks of Trebizond:—
He marks the sunlight as it paints
That glorious cloud of holy saints,
Until his shuddering spirit faints;
For, though he sees that heaven of saints,
There is no other heaven beyond!

VII.

He hears the golden gust and rush
Of rich and mellow organ thunder,
Now winding heavenward in a gush
Of swelling praise and holy wonder,
Now falling, with a soft rebound,
Rolling deep basses round and round;
Till fluted notes again aspire
In lark-like dartings;—from the choir,

With upward flutterings, higher and higher,
One note rich-throbbing in desire
Goes giddy in a whirl of fire
Up shuddering solitudes of sound;
   And then returning,
   Earthward yearning,
Lo! the luted music falls
Soft as water down the walls
Of sparry grottos, underground;
Then, like sword-blades glancing brightly,
Plunge the sudden notes out lightly,
Till the treble swerves and skips,
And the muffled thunder, low
Rolling inward, heaves and dips,
Like a midnight sea-swell;—lo!
Clarion-bugles seem to blow,
And all the loosened grandeurs go
Rocking sweetly to and fro,
In a sumptuous overflow,
And throbbing harmonies kiss like lips :·
Still, amid the golden blare,
Rolling thunderous through the air
The bannered aisles about,
Like a curse flung into prayer,
Hears he hissing his wild doubt;
And he feels the holy chapel
Holier were, were he without.

PART III.

THE LITTLE BIRD.

I.

OUT from the books and stifling room,
Out of the shadows and the gloom,
Into the cloister-garden bright,
Into the summer air and light!

II.

He wanders in the humming breeze,
Amid the shadows of the trees,
Himself a shadow, ill at ease.

III.

When lo! from out a neighbouring copse,
With richest plumage sunny bright,
Making a wheel of coloured light,
A little bird, aflutter, drops
Down upon the pear-tree tops,
    Hopping lightly,
    Glancing brightly
'Mid the twisted, shadowy boughs,
Raining lightnings round his brows.

IV.

A glory and a wonder are
Its crested colours to the sight;
It shakes with music, as a star
Trembles with excess of light :
Round about its throat assemble
Blushes of the damask rose ;
And a deepening violet goes
Sleeking down its back, atremble ;
Rich and hazy flutterings
Glow about its yellow wings
Dancing golden in the light;
Like a crowd of singing sunbeams
Gleams the little vision bright.

V.

Tame it seems, too, as a bird
Born amid the tropics hushed,
Where no flower is ever crushed,
And no voice of man is heard ;—
Nothing but a gorgeous noon,
And a silent silken river,
And an endless, endless June
Sinking down into a swoon,
Or a low and bulging moon
For ever and for ever.

VI.

Up among the twigs it ran,
Hopping, wheeling, full of graces;
'Mid the apples with the tan
Summering all their jocund faces;
When the monk, advancing near it,
Strove to touch it with his finger,
Scarcely seemed the bird to fear it,
Only, with a sidelong linger,
Hopped it on—a twig or two—
All its purples in a shiver,
Shaking like a ruffled river
In the storm of notes it blew.

VII.

All along the garden alleys,
Past the dial on the lawn,
Followed he the happy sallies
Of this creature of the dawn,
Out, into the solitude
Of the summer-haunted wood.

VIII.

Out, amid the stirless hush
Of the twilight shadows dun,
Glancing on, from bush to bush,
Glowing like a burning blush,

Followed he, with cheek aflush,
This gleaming creature of the sun :—
On about three hundred paces
From the cloister-garden door,
Joined he in the wheeling races,
Through the copse and open spaces—
Sudden summer on their faces
As the branches backward bore—
Just about three hundred paces
From the little Gothic door,
Just three hundred, and no more!

IX.

When, behold! a slope of sunbeams
Smote athwart the inner gloom,
Steeping all the fluttering plumage
In a ruddier golden bloom ;
And the little bird went winging
Showering music down, like rain,
Up the slope of sunbeams, singing,
And he saw it not again!

PART IV.

THE RETURN.

I.

Young Urban, musing still, returned ;
His pious soul within him yearned,
As in the days of old, to pray ;
But still he clutched his misery.
"A thousand long-drawn years !" quoth he,
"I cannot—though I wish it—see
How centuries can roll away,
Muffled in silent mystery,
Just as a night-watch hushed, or be,
Even to God, but as a day !"

II.

Wonder of wonders ! as he spoke
A vision on his senses broke :
A mighty abbey met his eyes,
Just like his own, but thrice its size ;
And where, not half an hour before,
The little cloister-garden stood—
The garden with the Gothic door
That opened out upon the wood—
A huge cathedral rose on high,
Three-steepled ;—every vanèd spire

Flung up into the summer sky
Great shining spokes of steadfast fire!

III.

About the Abbey all was hushed,
Just as it was an hour before;
The corbels in the sunlight flushed,
The great east window glowed and blushed:—
He could not find the Gothic door:—
And where the sun-dial erst was seen
Rose a new wing above the wood,
And where the Abbot's house had been
A great refectory bulging stood,
And where the apples were, a flood
Of painted windows glimmered keen:—
And all the strange and mystic scene
Filled him with wonder where he stood.

IV.

All in amaze, he sought the door;
And as he stretched his hand to knock,
Behold! a pursy Sacristan—
Whom he had never seen before—
Descending from the steeple-clock,
No sooner saw him, than he ran
Pale with affright;—his starting eyes
Both wide agoggle, twice their size!

V.

Ho heard the noise of banging doors,
Sounding up long corridors,
"Deo gratias," quoth the Porter,
As he drew the bolt aside—
"Bene"—but ere it was uttered
On white lips the blessing died!

VI.

He sought the stately Chapter-hall,
Where the Brethren were assembled,
And he whispered—"Strangers all—
What a change an hour may make!"
As he bent his figure tall
Every limb among them trembled,
Every eye was seen to quake,
Every hand was seen to shake,
And he unfolded his brief tale
Unto listeners hushed and pale.

VII.

But, ere the narrative was told,
Through both his ears strange noises rung;
Ho felt his limbs were growing cold;
Ho shook with palsy, like the old;
Ho saw a silver beard had rolled
Down to his girdle, fold on fold—
The girdle where the keys were hung—

And all the keys, though almost new,
Looked red with rust, and worn out too.

VIII.

When lo! from out a grated case,
With tottering step, and blanched face,
A monk a written parchment bore,
Illumined all, and bright with gold
And costly crimson; and it told
How, just three hundred years before,
The young monk Urban first was missed,
And never had been heard of more!

IX.

Deep silence was there as he read—
Silence—and wonder—and great dread.
. Quoth the monk Urban, young no more,
Sighing deeply, "Ah I see!
Forest bird that sang to me
In the wondrous days of yore,
Mystic ages rolled away
As I watched thy happy play,
And the little Gothic door
Opened on eternity!
All my faith I owe to thee;
And, adoring God, I see
How a thousand years may be
Even as a single day!"

Then he bowed his reverend head :—
All the Fathers, gathering near,
Hushed their very breath to hear
Every word that might be said :—
Quoth the Abbot shortly—" Brethren,
Back to prayers—he is dead ! "

O LITTLE CHILD:

In Memoriam.

O LITTLE child! that camest, and art gone,
Whose tiny footprints are upon our hearts;
O little wonder of the dreaming eyes,
Whose dreams we saw not, and could never see;
Who wert with us, and yet we knew thee not,
Nor thought that, underneath our quiet roof,
An angel harboured with us for a time,
And was our child, and is our child no more,
Being familiar with the floor of heaven,
And dwelling nigh unto the throne of God!
Dost ever think of us, as we of thee?
Dost ever bend thy beaming brow, O child!
Only a little space—a little space—
And turn from all the glories of thy home
To look into the lorn hearts thou hast left?

And we, O child! who tend our daily tasks,
Go in and out, and weep with those who weep,
And laugh with those who laugh, and buy and sell,
And travel o'er the dusty highways still
As though thou wert not, and hadst never been,
As when we knew thy little sunny face

Would surely greet us at the garden-gate;—
Dost think that we forget thee, O our child?

Not always are we in the weary mart;
Not always are we plodding in the streets.
We, in our rural home, when the grey dusk
Falls upon copse and meadow, saunter out,
And do not talk, but think of thee, O child!
And, in the night, when heavy hearts are hushed,
In the deep night we hear the beating rain,
And in the beating rain the wailing wind,
And in the wailing wind a cry, a low,
Soft cry, not as of agony, but bliss—
A silvery cry, as though we heard a thrill
Of spirit-music, far beyond the rain,
Beyond the wailings of the wind, beyond
The storms and gloomy reaches of the night,—
Out of the golden spaces far beyond.
And then we dream. We do but dream, O child!
O little child! that camest, and art gone,
That wert our child, and art our child no more,
We dream thou hast not yet forgotten us,
But yearnest from thy starry home, as we
Yearn towards the heavens for thee. We do but
        dream,
And in our dreamings are not quite forlorn.

Thy room is here, sweet babe! We enter it—
The room, but oh! the child. Thy little bed

Is white in moonlight;—Oh! for the beauteous form.
Thy toys are trembling in our palms—but oh!
The tiny, dimpled hands that fingered them.
The stairs are here;—but oh! the little feet.
Gone! Gone for ever! Yet we hope to reach
The heaven that holds thee; and, with humble hearts,
Thank God for thee, O child! We know that thou
Art seeing now, and not as in a dream,
The things we long for, and shall never see
Until we join thee in the after-world;—
Thee, little child! who camest, and art gone,
Who wert *our* child, and art our child no more,
Being familiar with the floor of heaven,
And dwelling nigh unto the throne of God!

ZARA.

I.

Six years have passed, since from her mountain-home
Zara came down to Delhi;—six bright years
Since first her great eyes flashed on tower and dome
Through gushes of hot tears.
Oh! how she gazed from that high mountain-peak,
When on the far horizon's utmost rim
The royal city shimmered far and dim
Between the earth and heaven,—a purple streak
Betwixt the green and gold; a dusky band
Of elephants went wavering o'er the land,
Gaudy with trappings, but so faint and far
Their silver buckles, flashing like a star,
Glowed larger than themselves: she drank the scene
As one who bids farewell to what has been
Once and for ever, and so passes on
Into the future, with far-straining eyes,
Wondering what next, and saying amid sighs
O'er all the old familiars, "Dead and gone!"
But now she has been taught no more to look
With stag-eyed wonder on the stranger's face,
And, with the rapid instincts of her race,
Has learnt her maiden lessons by the book;

Is coy as any in the drawing-room,
Is still and stately, or is maiden-meek;
Can sigh and simper o'er a lover's doom,
Or in hot blushes thrill with gorgeous bloom
The tawny marble of her Indian cheek;
She sings and dances, plays on the guitar,
Knits and embroiders, makes her morning calls,
Rustles her silks, and asks you how you are,
And, ere you answer, rattles on of balls;
Is in all things, save what you cannot tell,
A sweet brunette, a fashionable *belle*.
But in the silence of her lonely room,
When none are by to listen or to mark,
She flings aside her dresses in the dark,
And with them her reserve.   She beats the gloom
In frenzied passion, all her tropic hate
Gathered in lurid lustres in her eyes,
Her savage nature glowing *sans* disguise,
A stormy Nemesis,—a dusky Fate.
All the affronts and trifles, which by day
She carols over, merry as a lark,
By night the wounded tigress makes her prey,
And paws and crunshes them within the dark,
Her terrible beauty pallid with her ire,
And her large eyeballs flaming o'er with fire.

II.

The dance is almost done,
And laguidly the dancers move;

L

Already coos the early dove,
Already all the east begins to glow
With mellow morning-tints; and, lo!
Yonder the morning sun!
The lamps are paling in the rooms,
And now o'er minaret and spire
And hushed pagoda, runs a thrill of fire,
And rosy flush of blooms.
Long threads of morning light
Are woven on the ruddy mountain-peaks;
The dawn is here with all his gleesome freaks,
Painting with gold and amber streaks
The dark face of the gloom,
And flinging unbought favours down
On nooks and corners of the town,
On palace, tower, and tomb.
And all night long, through all the mazes of the dance,
Have Walter Verner and sweet Alice Grey
Been burning in the fierce and furtive glance
Of Zara far away.
Sullenly has she answered every call
To join the revelry,
And kept her seat behind the thickest fall
Of Persian tapestry;
Darting her arrowy looks along the room,
Across the giddy swim
Of silks and muslins, and of tresses dim,
Amid their topaz and their ruby bloom,
Searching alone for him.

Alone, amid that music, mirth, and sheen,
He has the power to thrill her inmost heart,
To bid the dusky goddess play her part,
And be once more a Queen;
To flame her passionate beauty on the sight,
And be the Cleopatra of the night;
But not a look amid the endless dance
Has answered Zara's dark and passionate glance;
And hence her anger, hence her frequent sigh,
And hence the leaping lightning in her eye.
Ah! let the glad and golden music roll,
It will not soothe the trouble of her soul,
It will not tame the fierceness of her frown,
Though in sweet gushes it go up in prayer,
With passionate pleading hands into the air,
With musical sighs and moanings of despair,
To bring the infinite down.
She has no sighs to throw away
On aught, save Walter and sweet Alice Grey.

All through that weary, weary night,
Heavy with musky odours, filled with light,
Glad with a hundred voices, gay with wit,
Thrilling with music, droll with sparkling fun,
Flashing with riches rare,—
Alone in her great beauty will she sit,
Catching the wavy glory in her hair,
Flinging the brightness back with many an angry
    glare,

And wishing all were done.
For what to her are music, mirth, and wine ?
What all this blaze of beauty but an empty sign ?
What all this glorious talk, though half divine,
But idle air ?
A worship offered at a godless shrine,—
A garlanded despair.

He is no longer hers,—but was he ever ?
A low, wild, silver laugh rang through the room,
And then a thrilling whisper,—"Never, never!"
Startled the dancers like the breath of doom;
But soon the fearless English bloom
Into the ladies' cheeks came back, crimson and glad
        as ever.
Aye, let her ponder !   She will never find
Aught more than this to soothe her angry mind—
" Walter was always generous, always kind,
But nothing more,
And nothing more,—ah! nothing more
Will he now be to her, for ever and for ever!"

Henceforth her heart and life are lorn,
Henceforth the world is dim,—
Its sunny tresses soiled or shorn,
Its banners of beauty draggled and torn,
Its bridal blushes wan and worn,
For she is nought to him.

His heart is in his eyes agleam,—
His honest heart, as open as day!—
Its love is all for Alice Grey,
For her, oh! not a beam.

ONLY A LITTLE HOUSE.

———

ONLY a little house—
A house by the side of a hill—
With dances of sunshine gleaming about
Through tossing branches in and out,
And the sound of a little rill,
That, through the tiny garden-plot,
All day long, and all night through,
Murmurs music ever new,—
"I am happy—and you?
Why not?"

Only a little house,
But a house brimful of life,—
Busy husband, and happy wife,
Prattle of babies three :
Singing of birds, and humming of bees ;
Shadow and sunshine on the trees ;
Glancing needles, eager talk ;
Books, and pens, and the evening walk
Through the meadows down below ;—
Thus the summer days go by,
And we look on, and only sigh—
We sigh, but do not know.

Only a little house,
But a house heart-full of bliss,—
Plenty of work, and plenty of play ;
Busy heart and brain all day ;
And then, ere the good-night kiss
The lingering shadow of worldly care,
Wafted off by the evening prayer ;
And silence falls on the little house,
Save for the whir of the midnight mouse,
Here, and there, and everywhere ;
And through the tiny garden-plot,
The voice of the rill, which, all night through,
Murmurs its music ever new,—
"I am happy—and you ?
Why not ?"

Happy ! O little house !
House by the side of the hill,
Who can say what an hour may bring ?
Who would think that the song we sing
Is the music of coming ill ?
Little it boots to live and learn
Lessons harsh and lessons stern ;
Rather turn to the merry notes
Of the voice that ever floats
Through the flowery garden-plot,
All day long and all night through,
With its burden ever new,—

" I am happy—and you ?
Why not?"

Only a little house—
But a house all still and cold,—
Gone the voice of the happy child ;
Gone the smile of the matron mild ;
Gone the summer-gold
That fell on the gables one by one ;
Gone the human toil and care ;
The daily task, the evening prayer ;
Father, and mother, and babes—all gone !
And, through the roof, I hear the rain
Dripping on the desolate floor,
And hear the creaking of a door
No human hand shall shut again,
And hear a murmur harsh go by
Through the tangled garden-plot,
Where the ragged palings rot,—
" I am wretched, I know not why ;
Would you live, or would you die ?"

YAN OR TWO LILE BITS I' T' FURNESS DIALECT.

I.

AULD GRANFADDER JONES.

Auld Granfadder Jones is stordy and strang;
Auld Granfadder Jones is six feet lang;
He hes spindle shanks, he hes lantern jaws,
But there's neabody's laugh like his hee-haws!
He's first at a weddin' an' last at a fair,
He's t' jolliest of aw, whaiver is there;
For he keeps a lad's heart in his wizened auld skin,
An' warks out his woes as fast as they're in;
Ye'd niver believe he'd iver seen trouble,
Though there's times when t'auld fellow's amaist
    walking double;
He hes corns on his taes, an' t' gout i' his hands,
An' he shivers an' shacks wheniver he stands,
He hes t' rheumatiz tu; but whaiver heeard groans
Frae t' withered auld lips o' Granfadder Jones?

II.

T' AULD MAN.

T' auld man! T' auld man!
He's eighty year an' mair;

He wrought sœan, wrought leate,
Wrought hard an' sair;
An' now he sits i' t' sunshine,
Duing aw he can;
Wha wod grudge him house-room?
Poor auld man!

Lang afoore we saaw t' leet,
He was fashing hard;
Indure, out o' dure,
I' shuppen, field, an' yard;
Lang afoore we saaw t' leet,
He was hoddin t' plough—
He wrought hard for us, lads,
We'se du t' saame now
For t' auld man i' t' sunshine,
Duing aw he can;
Wha wod grudge him house-room?
Poor auld man!
Aw thro' t' summer sunshine
He watches t' clouds gang by;
Nin can tell what wonders
Glour up in his eye;
For far-off, an' far-off
Aw his leeaks gang,
Thro' many summer sunshines
To t' times when he was strang,
An' laboured leate an' early
Wi' hoe, an' speade, an' plough,

An' dud his best for us, lads,
As we are duing now
For t' auld man i' t' sunshine,
Duing aw he can ;—
Wha wod grudge him house-room?
Poor auld man!

III.

LILE POLLY.

Ir's nobbut this time last year, come tomorn,
Sen me an' Polly walkt to U'ston fair,
Across t' green fields an' down t' lang sunny looans,
A good three mile an' mair.
We stopp't a' parlish bit tu, now an' then,
An' yet it mod a' been three yirds,
For t' time flang by at sic a reate,
Titter nor wings o' birds.
For sweet lile Polly was wi' me ;
But now my heart is sair,
For I'se see Polly, bonny Polly,
Niver, niver mair!

I'd often hid behint a dike,
Or ligged in an empty cart
To leeak at her, an' hear her sing,—
An' t' sound o' her bonny voice wod ring
An' finger about my heart.
I darn't tell her what I felt,

But leeakt an' leeakt an' niver stirr'd,
Though I'd a' geen my silver watch
Just for ya single word.
Oh! sweet lile Polly! Bonny Polly!
Oh! my heart is sair;
For I'se see Polly, gentle Polly,
Niver, niver mair!

Afaoore we gat to U'ston town,
I pluckt up heart an' spak reet out;
She leeakt at me—the sweet lile lass—
But what she answered matters nout.
I'se niver forgit the words she spak
Under that goolden sky;
A limmer, bouny fairy she,
An' a gurt clodhopper I!
But niver heed; she loved me weell;
That's a' I care to knaw;
An' it's gang wi' me, baith neet an' day,
Through sun, an' winter snaw.
Oh! sweet lile Polly, bonny Polly,
Oh! my heart is sair;
For I'se see Polly, gentle Polly,
Niver, niver mair!